All in the Family

FAITH ISSUES FOR FAMILIES DEALING WITH ADDICTION

RITA B. HAYS

WestBow
PRESS

WestBow Press books may be ordered through booksellers or by contacting:

WestBow Press
A Division of Thomas Nelson
1663 Liberty Drive
Bloomington, IN 47403
www.westbowpress.com
1-(866) 928-1240

Because of the dynamic nature of the Internet, any Web addresses or links contained in this book may have changed since publication and may no longer be valid. The views expressed in this work are solely those of the author and do not necessarily reflect the views of the publisher, and the publisher hereby disclaims any responsibility for them.

ISBN: 978-1-4497-0229-8 (sc)
ISBN: 978-1-4497-0230-4 (hc)
ISBN: 978-1-4497-0228-1 (e)

Library of Congress Control Number: 2010928774

Printed in the United States of America

WestBow Press rev. date: 7/5/2010

This book is dedicated to my husband Bill:

Together, with God's help, we have walked this journey of addiction.

Our faith and love have sustained us, making us stronger for the journey of life that lies ahead. Thanks for your amazing strength, bold courage, unwavering loyalty, and your support and confidence.

Contents

INTRODUCTION

As a United Methodist pastor, I encountered many families in the congregations I served who faced addictions. While I sympathized with these families and sought to offer them my support, I had no idea what their lives were like, day in and day out, as they dealt with addiction.

Now I know. Now I understand. Now I am able not only to minister as a pastor, but also to relate to them as a fellow traveler along the slippery, twisting road of addiction.

My personal family life was turned upside down when addiction entered my home. Addiction brought me up close and personal with evil. Addiction forced my family to question God's presence against our sense of abandonment and isolation. Addiction challenged us to evaluate our relationship with God and with other believers. Guilt, worry, blame, and the hopelessness associated with addiction brought us to our knees, but even in our humble postures, we wondered if our prayers really mattered. As Christian believers, my family and I immediately searched for written materials that might help us deal with the faith issues we had encountered as a result of addiction. We found very few available to help us, as persons of faith, to deal with our struggles involving spiritual matters.

As I talked with other families facing addiction, I recognized that they too were searching for tools to help them deal with the paralyzing effects of addiction. They questioned where God was in the midst of their family struggles. They wondered how they should pray and where they could turn in the Scriptures for guidelines and survival techniques. They wanted assurance that the guilt, the worry, and the blame, primarily caused by their enabling habits, would eventually diminish. Above all else, they needed affirmation that somehow, in the chaos and the insanity of addiction, they could muster enough faith to dispel the gloomy, dark chambers of addiction and replace them with the radiant light of hope.

This book was written to address the faith issues with which families wrestle when addiction enters their homes. I have not sought to gloss over the devastating consequences of addiction in family life, neither have I refrained from painting a picture of the truly demonic nature of addiction. If there is any shred of hope to be found in our addiction journeys, we will not find our solutions by shrinking away from the truth. Rather, we discover peace, gain sanity, embrace hope, and strengthen our relationship with God and others only when we can look addiction squarely in the eye and see its evil powers honestly revealed. Addiction manifests itself as a menacing, vicious disease that works to destroy our families and our faith. However, armed with the resources of our faith, we can stand as courageous believers.

As I write these words, I dwell in the season of Lent, the time of the wilderness experience for Christians as we make our faith journeys that ultimately intersect us with the cross of Christ. We know the painful experience of living in the barren wilderness of addiction. We bear heroically our crosses of addictions on a daily basis, constantly living in the gripping fear that the weights of them are too great and that our burdens will destroy us. Yet, we must be reminded that beyond Lent, the wilderness, and the cross awaits Easter, new life, and resurrection. God did not open the door of the tomb, raise Christ from the dead, and offer us new life in vain. God rolled the stone away on that first Easter morning in demonstration of God's power to remove the stones that hinder our faith. Just on the other side of death is resurrection. Just on the other side of addiction is new life. Our task as people of faith, in this difficult Lenten season of our lives, is to journey beyond the wilderness of addiction, beyond the cross of addiction, and beyond the tomb of addiction to feast our hungry, weary eyes upon the bright new morning that awaits us in recovery.

Rita B. Hays
Season of Lent 2009
Nashville, Tennessee

CHAPTER ONE:

I Believe. How Did This Happen to Me?

"Even though I walk through the darkest valley, I fear no evil, for you are with me ..."

Psalms 23:4a (NRSV)

Those of us who face the ravaging disease of addiction know what it is like to walk through the darkest valley. Addiction turned our family life upside down, spun us out of control, tore our family members apart, and collapsed our normalcy into shambles. The tornado of addiction swept into our family, leaving behind a wide trail of destruction. Now, faced with unmanageable situations, we struggle to know how to pick up the pieces, clean up the debris, and establish any semblance of sanity in our family life. After all, we have been deceived by, manipulated by, and betrayed by a person we dearly loved. Addiction has sucked the dignity, integrity, and confidence from our addict, leaving a shell of the person we once knew. A family disease—addiction—without a pang of remorse or a measure of mercy, led both addict and family members into a valley with no flicker of light, the valley of the shadow of death.

Plunged into this dark valley, addiction forces us to come face to face with issues of our faith if we are to have any hope of restored sanity. Guilt-ridden ourselves, we question God's role in our unmanageable lives. We call ourselves people of faith. We believed and trusted in a God of power and might. Yet, addiction seems to hold the upper hand, yielding a powerful force, demonic in nature. Time and again, we fell on bended knee, humbled by a force beyond our control. Surely God saw us amid our tears, praying, clinging to a thin thread of hope and grasping for a word of grace. In the midst of the dark valley, surely, we of all people have earned the right to ask some questions, have we not? So we ask them, honestly, without reserve.

> **"Is God even in our family addiction picture?"**
>
> **"If I am a person of faith, why is this not only happening to my family, but consuming my family?"**
>
> **"If I had been a better parent, a better spouse, a better child, then could I have done something to prevent this horrible disease from inflicting itself upon my loved one?"**
>
> **"Where is faith in the abandonment of addiction?"**

The psalmist assures us of God's abiding presence in the midst of our family addiction. Psalm 23 paints the picture of a God who cares deeply for His children, especially when they walk through the darkest valleys of life. The darkest valleys were actual places in the biblical setting of our psalm. Some of the canyons were so steep that sunlight could not penetrate the bottom of the canyons. Shepherds called any such canyon "the valley of the shadow of death," due to the darkness and lack of sunlight.

The psalmist tells us that there is no place of darkness in our lives, no dangerous place in our lives, where God is not present. In our addiction journey, we do not walk alone. Our Good Shepherd walks beside us, strengthening us each step of the unknown journey. God will never forsake us. The psalmist goes on to say that "God is our refuge and strength, a very present help in trouble" (Psalms 46:1, NRSV). God is present with us, right now, wherever this journey has taken us, and God will remain with us.

Be assured of God's love for each of us. The biblical picture is one of a God who never gives up on His children. As individuals created in God's image, God offers each of us a covenant of love and grace. As a child of God, our addicts dwell in the realm of His covenant of love and grace, for he or she is also created in God's image. God is working in the life of our addict, whether he or she recognizes or acknowledges God's presence. God continually works in our family life, granting healing, grace, and strength. Just when we think we cannot face another day of betrayal and manipulation, God provides the gifts and the tools of wisdom, courage, and strength.

We serve a God who controls our world and our lives. If we do not believe this, we struggle alone, exhausted, finally submitting ourselves to the powerful forces of addiction and giving evil permission to gain the upper hand. By doing so, we come to experience defeat in our lives. As God's people, loved and claimed by our Parent God, we must never give up hope, even when the situation seems hopeless.

This does not mean that we meekly stand by and watch our addict destroy his or her life. Some of us have faced situations where our addict stole from us, physically abused us, punched holes in our walls, and threatened our safety. Worry became a constant companion as we watched our financial resources dwindle. We poured out money like it was water. Money was generously and freely given, time and again, as we sought professional help for our addict or provided him or her the means to enter rehab center after rehab center.

Finally, a time came where some of us saw no other alternative than to ask our addict to leave our house, where we felt forced to cut off financial support, or where our own personal safety required calling the police to have our addict arrested. These decisions were not easy to make and were not made lightly on our part. Yet, somewhere in the depth of our being, God gave us the strength to make these decisions so the healing process in our family circle could begin. Know that even in these difficult choices, God was present with us, providing us with wisdom and discernment. Each of these valleys of darkness was a place where God remained faithfully beside us, offering sustaining grace, love, and care.

In the middle of crisis after crisis, day after day of drama, night after night of sleeplessness and worry, God dwelt with us. Perhaps we perceived God to be far removed from us because we did not "feel" or sense God's presence. Sometimes, all we felt was emptiness and utter despair. We should not be too hard on ourselves. What we have been through would amaze most people, even elicit sympathy and pity from a few; frankly, most would find our story so far-fetched and unbelievable, they would think we had to be making it up. We must not underestimate what a toll addiction has taken on our family members and us. The tangled web of addiction draws us in completely and holds us totally in its powerful grip. Courage and strength are the tools we must draw upon within ourselves to begin the restoration process, and only God can truly offer these gifts to us. In our questioning and searching for answers, we may have forgotten the physical, mental, emotional, and spiritual drain this disease has taken on our lives. We must examine ourselves and be totally honest as we admit that this disease is far more powerful than we ever imagined and far more damaging to our well-being than we might wish to confess.

During those restless nights and ceaseless days of the unknown, our families rested in the security of God's love, even if we neglected to recognize God's presence or sense God's care. God works in our lives, often in mysterious ways, ways we cannot begin to understand or explain. Many times, we have failed to comprehend how closely the shadow of the Almighty abides within us. Many incidents in our lives are a result of God's divine intervention and outside the realm of human explanation. God comes to us as Parent God, walking closely with us through our valley of the shadow of death. We acknowledge God as comforting companion when we open ourselves up to the Spirit of God working within our lives. Looking back now, we may recall many times when God was present, but we were so caught up in the vicious cycle of addiction that we did not even give Him a moment of our day. Do not fret about this: God understands our anxieties, our worries, and our constant occupation with our addict's care. Go ahead now and accept the gift of God's love and faithfulness offered in the past, present, and future.

Even when friends, co-workers, family members, and our addict turn their backs on us and question our decisions, God stays with us. God never leaves our side for one moment. God sticks with us through the legal battles, the family visits to the rehab centers, or the trips to see our addict in jail. God dwells within us in our useless but loving attempts to help our addict by pouring out bottles of alcohol, pleading with our addict not to go to the drug dealer, and trying to talk sense into our addict until we are exhausted. God's intimate relationship with us results in God knowing the excruciating pain of having our loved one tell us that he or she loves the drug of choice more than he or she loves us.

God goes with us when we drive our addict hundreds of miles to his or her rehab center, hoping this time he or she "gets it" and will finally accept recovery as a way of life. God keeps watch over us when we sit in a hospital room after our addict has been in a bad car accident or when our addict faces hospitalization from abusing his or her drug of choice.

Never forget that God constantly walks with our addicts—our beloved spouse, our beloved child, or our beloved family member. God walks with them in their valleys of the shadow of death. They belong to God as beloved children of God. No matter what actions they choose, they will always be beloved children of God. God goes with them to the drug dealer's house, God sits with them in the recovery meetings, God holds their hands when they shake from alcohol withdrawals, and God rejoices with them in any decision they make that puts them on the road toward recovery. However, because God loves them so much, He allows them free will to make choices that may ultimately break our hearts—and His heart.

Know—without a doubt—that nothing separates our family members, our addicts, or ourselves from God's love. The apostle Paul speaks confidently of God's abiding presence with us at all times and in all circumstances. In the biblical book of Romans, Paul boldly and confidently asks the question:

> *"Who will separate us from the love of Christ? Will hardship, or distress, or persecution, or famine, or nakedness, or peril, or sword?" For I am convinced that neither death, nor life, nor angels, nor rulers, nor things present, nor things to come, nor powers, nor height, nor depth, nor anything else in all creation, will be able to separate us from the love of God in Christ Jesus our Lord."*
>
> *Romans 8:35 (NRSV)*

Paul states emphatically that absolutely nothing in this present life and the life to come can separate us from the love of God expressed to us in Jesus Christ. If Paul had known anything of our struggles with addiction, he would not hesitate to add "addiction" to his list of those difficult challenges that cannot separate us from God's love. We always remain secure and anchored in God's love, regardless of the whirlwind of addiction.

Even if we understand, without a doubt, that God loves us and walks with us on the addiction journey, we must confess that unresolved issues gnaw away at us. As people of faith, we simply fail to comprehend how this could happen to our family. Maybe we regularly attend church or even serve as leaders in our communities of faith. We might describe ourselves as "serious students of the Bible" or "prayer warriors." We also proudly admit that our family members are devout believers who sincerely care for the needs of others. We have always tried to do what is right and just, and apply godly principles in our everyday living. We have taught and reinforced these principles in our family life. What went wrong? Is God punishing us? Did God cause this to happen to our family?

Addressing these questions begins honestly, by understanding that addiction is a disease and not a choice. In the past, addiction was viewed by society as a moral issue. Now, clear evidence from the medical community ultimately destroys the notion that addicts can just stop if they really cared about themselves and their families. They cannot stop once the disease of addiction progresses; the brain becomes wired in such a way that makes it impossible for our addict to simply put down his bottle or stop using her drugs. We have discovered that pleading with our addicts to stop has led to a dead end. Our threats and our constant nagging have not worked either. Many addicts, propelled into the black hole of addiction, find no escape. They discover incredible means to feed their habits and continue even if their actions risk alienating family members and result in divorce, legal battles, and run-ins with the law.

Remember that this "monster" is not the person we married, the child we raised, or the parent we trusted. Addiction turns a competent, smart, well-groomed "Dr. Jekyll" into a cursing, angry, unkempt, and sometimes violent "Mr. Hyde." Our addict wakes up each day in bondage, held captive by a powerful force beyond his or her—and our—power to control.

We must remove the blame of addiction off of our shoulders. Even if our family has a history of addiction and we can name addicts in the family's past, we should not impose guilt for the disease on our family. Statistics certainly point overwhelmingly to the potential of a person becoming an addict if there is a family history of the disease. Yet we waste time and keep ourselves from finding healing for our family and our addicts when we spend time focusing blame on the family tree. We must free ourselves from thinking we could have done anything to prevent this disease. Our addicts suffer from a devastating disease for which there is no cure. Most addicts will live with this disease until the day they die. Recovery offers the addict hope to live a clean, sober life.The steps the addict takes while in recovery do not cure the disease, but instead, help the addict to better manage his or her addiction. Our addict must surrender himself or herself to a rigorous, diligent program of recovery. Recovery takes place daily and is a lifetime commitment.

One of the groups that offer support to families of alcoholics fervently states a truth important for families of addicts to remember: "You did not cause it, you cannot control it, and you cannot cure it." No, we did not cause it by anything we said, did, did not say, and did not do. We must quit trying to second-guess ourselves when it comes to our family role in addiction. Our addict's body and mind were predisposed to this disease so that the risk of addiction became a reality when our addict first picked up a bottle of alcohol or tried a drug. When they continually used the drug of choice, they often found themselves addicted. As much as we try, families cannot control it, a lesson we learned through our wasted attempts. No, we cannot cure this disease, but we can guide and offer the addict the chance at recovery.

My husband is an engineer. He always thought that somehow he could control and "fix" the addict in our family. Engineers fix things in their profession, so my husband was totally frustrated and overwhelmed that he could not fix our addict. Finally, he came to the stark realization that he could not control or fix this disease, a reality that each of us dealing with addiction discover eventually. Confronting this truth head-on is difficult, but only by doing so can we begin the healing process in our family life. After my family accepted this truth, we were able to step aside and let God take control of our addict. We placed him in God's hands and in the hands of others in his recovery program. Where we had grossly failed, these experts and fellow addicts could help him. As hard as it was, we had to step aside and let our addict discover his own program of recovery.

As a pastor, I also thought I could fix the addict in our family. For some time, I thought I could work my family member's program of recovery for him. I constantly drove him to meetings, checked for hidden bottles around the house, and became his alarm clock for appointments. Sorry to brag, but I did an excellent job of working his program for him! But the harder I worked, the sicker he got. Our addict is now in a recovery program, working with a wise sponsor. He listens and obeys the advice of this sponsor as if his life depends on it—and it does! If our addicts are in recovery programs, let them work their own programs. Offer support, but stay out of the way. Most programs of recovery contain a spiritual dimension; the addict learns to submit his or her will to God (or a higher power). We need to give our addicts to God, knowing that just as we did not cause or control this disease, we cannot cure it, for we are not God.

What we can control is getting help for our families. The first time I attended a support group for families of addicts, I came away angry and resentful. The person speaking that day had the audacity to tell me that I needed to work a program of recovery for myself. She indicated that the best way to help my addict was to get myself well. She explained that I too was sick. She shared that addiction sickens the entire family. *What nonsense!* I thought. *I am not the addict. How ridiculous and insulting to tell me that I must work a program of recovery.* When I told my husband how disgusted I was with this meeting, he calmed me down and told me this speaker was right. He had been attending another similar support group and had gotten the same advice.

Do not take this as an insult, but a truth: Families of addicts, due to the toll of addiction, become sick people too. I would characterize us as wonderful enablers who are spiritually, physically, emotionally, and often financially drained. Our bodies and our spirits are worn out and totally exhausted. Our emotions run the gamut of panic, anxiety, fear, hope, and disappointment. Therefore, until we submit to a program of recovery, we cannot help our addicts recover. Even if our addict has not agreed to enter recovery and still continues to abuse his or her body, we must dedicate ourselves to finding recovery for our family. We do this by seeking out support groups and resources in the community that offer a plan of recovery that fits our family's needs.

We must remain adamant about our recovery, giving recovery a priority in our lives. We cannot let anything stand in the way of working our own programs of healing. When we find ourselves putting work responsibilities, family obligations, friends' objections, acquaintances' criticism, or our addict's refusal to get help ahead of our recovery, we will fail in our efforts. Recovery must take first place in our lives, second only to our faith in God. As impractical as this may sound to us, there is no easy route to recovery. Our family's recovery will take time, hard work, and diligent effort on our part.

Certainly, looking back, we recognize the mistakes we made. These mistakes enabled our addict to keep using, and we find ourselves guilt-ridden. In the next chapter, we will address the problem of guilt, but we can start by giving our guilt and our shame over to God. Having done this, we are freed to seek healthy ways of recovery for our addict and our family members. We should learn all we can about the disease of addiction. Our time is well spent researching ways to guide our addict to a recovery community that matches his or her needs. Seek qualified facilities and centers that are capable of addressing his or her addiction problems.

Given the nature of the disease, we should not be surprised that addiction causes upheaval in our family life. Addiction is a selfish disease; it turns our addicts into self-centered people who only care about one thing: their drug of choice. Addiction is a manipulative disease: it forces our addicts to lie, cheat, steal, and break the law if necessary to feed the addiction. Addiction is a consuming disease: it robs our addicts of their dignity, strips away all honesty, and leaves our addicts as persons we hardly recognize. Of course, nothing I am saying comes as a surprise. I reiterate what we already know in order to help us to understand the evil nature of the disease of addiction.

My husband and I are people of faith who believe in a loving God, a God of grace. Never once in our loved one's struggle with addiction did we blame God or view his disease as punishment for our wrongdoing. That does not mean we have not yielded and been blindsided by the powerful, demonic force this disease has wrought upon our family. We are both Christian believers who worship in a mainline denomination. I would describe our theology as moderate and middle of the road. Although we acknowledged the presence of evil in our world, we rarely talked about demons in a personal manner. Now we struggle to understand the amount of evil we saw concentrated in our loved one's life. The longer and harder our addict was sucked into the black hole of addiction, the stronger evil's grip became on this child of God. How powerful is addiction versus God? My husband and I agreed that the existence of evil, concentrated in one place—in the life of our addict and our family—was the most demonically powerful force we had ever seen. Our experience of evil shattered our notion of demonic forces as being alien to our sophisticated world view and our intellectual mindset.

Our modern world does not take evil seriously at times. Evil looked our family squarely in the face; we saw evil in specific, concrete terms. Our sterile, tidy picture of evil was swept away. No longer was *evil* just a vocabulary word we could define in general terms, a dusty concept found in a seminary textbook and brushed aside as some archaic, irrelevant notion. Society rightly condemns evil in conditions such as the horror of the Holocaust or the unjust and hateful actions of the Ku Klux Klan. These and other tragic events in history were so horrendous that we categorize them as the crucible of evil, so much so that we hesitate to speak of evil as a present reality in our everyday life. By doing this, at least in the area of addiction, we blame God or try to rationalize the disease in other ways.

God is more powerful than the evil forces of addiction, but we must never forget the demonic nature of this disease. The addict—and his or her family members—can never let their guards down for one moment. This disease is too tricky, too deceitful, too vicious, and cannot be trusted for even a second. At one point in our loved one's addiction, he related to us that the disease seemed to have a power of its own that controlled him. He described the disease as talking to him, especially during the times in which he tried to stay clean. From our addict's viewpoint, the disease wanted to destroy his life, it wanted him dead. I relate this story to clarify that addiction strikes a person with a vengeance. The temptation to continue to use was so great, beyond the control of our family member, and his was a daily struggle to resist.

For this reason, a program of recovery for our addicts and family members must contain a spiritual dimension. For recovery to succeed, we must turn our lives over to God and admit that through this disease, our lives have become totally unmanageable and insane. Only God can restore us to sanity. Trust Him, believing that as we turn our lives over to the will of God, He is working to restore our families to a place of sanity. Addiction has wreaked enough havoc on our lives. With God's help, the time is now: You are now ready to begin the healing process.

So where does this leave us in our faith journey? The psalmist declares, *"Even though I walk through the darkest valley, I fear no evil, for you are with me ..." Psalms 23:4a (NRSV)*. Fear no evil? Surely, the psalmist must be kidding! Fear has been our daily companion on this journey of addiction. We fear addiction's zeal to destroy our addict, to destroy our family, and to destroy our sanity. We still fear the unknown, questioning will our addict choose recovery—or relapse? Addiction keeps us always on the edge of our seats. Addiction saddles us with the burdens of waiting and worrying. Promises made and not kept have turned us into doubters. Even if our addict remains sober for several years, we are afraid of a return to old habits.

Yet, the psalmist was not joking when admonishing us to fear no evil. The writer of Psalm 23 trusts in a God whose power is greater than that of evil. The psalmist urges us to break free from the captivity of fear. Our psalmist knows that God dwells with us in the unknown spaces and places of life. We sacrifice our fears to our God, who accepts them as a pleasing offering. God and God alone is the one powerful enough to deal with our fears. Given the evil nature of addiction, we have met our match when we try to fight this disease without divine intervention. Only God can lead us safety through the dark valley of addiction. We anchor our faith in a God who will not forsake us.

Our addict may choose recovery, and for this, we will be eternally grateful. Our addict may never choose recovery, but his or her refusal must not keep us from seeking recovery for ourselves. Regardless of what we face ahead on the twisting, bumpy, perilous road of addiction, we never walk this road alone. Sometimes God walks beside us. Sometimes He is ahead of us, and sometimes He is behind us. We are covered on all sides by God's love. We anchor our faith in Him, for our faith is the only anchor strong enough to withstand the fierce winds of addiction. The storm of addiction is no match for the calm waters of God's peace and abiding presence. Even in the midst of the raging storm, we are safety anchored in the harbor of His love and grace.

CHAPTER TWO:

The Family Guilt Trip

"And you shall bring to the priest, as your guilt-offering to the Lord, a ram without blemish from the flock, or its equivalent for a guilt-offering. The priest shall make atonement on your behalf before the Lord, and you shall be forgiven for any of the things that one may do and incur guilt thereby."

Leviticus 6:7(NRSV)

In this Old Testament passage, a guilt offering brought sincerely and honestly before the Lord apparently lifted the heavy burden of guilt. If families of addicts believed bringing sacrifices to God would ultimately lift the burden of guilt off of our shoulders, our altars of addiction would overflow with our guilt offerings. Many of us are filled with embarrassment and shame; we regret our past mistakes and wonder if we can ever be fully forgiven. Family secrets have remained hidden behind closed doors, because sharing our family struggles with outsiders often resulted in blank stares, whispered innuendos, and open-mouthed looks of disbelief. We categorized ourselves as failures and enablers. We played our family roles of codependency as outstanding performers on the stage of addiction. We became so addicted to our addict's disease; what we thought was loving action on our part only fed the fires of his or her addiction.

Too often, as members of a family with an addict, we start thinking that maybe we deserved the blame we heaped upon ourselves. Winners at the blame game, we mistakenly believed we earned our prizes of worry, doubt, and guilt. Why? Somehow, in the back of our minds, we are at fault. We claimed our awards of dark depression, spiritual insomnia, family rift, and future uncertainty. Beaten down, overwhelmed, discouraged, and ultimately outsmarted by the disease of addiction, we wore our guilt as a token of our failure. Over time, this badge of guilt fatigued our body and mind, broke our spirit, destroyed our family unity, and undermined our spiritual relationship with God.

The source of our guilt is easily identified but not so quickly alleviated. Only by naming our guilt can we begin to rid our families of the panic and anxiety guilt has placed upon us. Only by claiming our guilt can we sacrifice our guilt on the altar of God's grace and begin the healing process in our families. Only by sharing our guilt with God and others and accepting God's gift of forgiveness can we make any strides toward forgiving our addict and ourselves. Naming, claiming, and sharing our guilt sets us free to become forgiven children of God.

We begin our confessions by naming the source of guilt that all families of addicts hold in common: the game of enabling. We played that game with such fervor that our addict constantly ended up holding all of the cards. We gave our addict rent money so he or she would not be forced out onto the streets; we made excuses when the boss called inquiring why our addict missed work; we drove the addict to the drug house as a safety measure or, like workhorses, we nursed, fed, clothed, and babied our addict with all the strength we could muster. Some of us were accommodating to the point of allowing ourselves to be physically abused. We admit that at times we were afraid of our addict and fearful of how our addict would survive without our help. Others felt such a strong bond of love toward our addict, a connection where we found ourselves chained in an unhealthy enabler/dependent relationship. Therefore, we piled guilt upon our heads even when we knew we acted out of love.

Looking back, we remember situation after situation in which our enabling allowed our addict to continue in his or her addictive ways. One woman shared her enabling method very effectively and poignantly when she described carrying a pillow around to place under her addict to keep him from falling and injuring himself. To her, this pillow was a vibrant symbol of her enabling and of her continued inability to let her addict do anything for himself. She surrendered to his beck and call twenty-four hours a day. She stood by, like his servant, ready to wait on his every need, any time he called—and even when he did not need her help. Her life centered on her addict. Even when she knew in her mind that what she was doing was wrong, she could not stop.

To those outside the circle of addiction, our enabling seems absolutely *crazy* and *unthinkable*; to us, it seemed perfectly *normal* and *reasonable*. The sound advice of friends fell on deaf ears. In some instances, we grew weary of individuals who had no clue at all about addiction. We became frustrated with their lack of experience. Despite that, they had plenty of answers for our dilemma and offered them without discretion. Often, their solutions were ill-advised; at other times, they were wise suggestions that we needed to heed. We lived with guilt for not listening; we lived with guilt for listening. We lived in guilt for our actions of enabling; we lived in guilt for the consequences we imposed.

Many of us made the difficult decision to stop the enabling at some point. The scenario might be that we quit giving our addict money, we ask our addict to leave our house, we have our addict arrested, or we divorce our addict. We came to the point where we had to impose consequences on our addict. Rather than alleviating the guilt, however, our efforts to stop enabling heaped more guilt upon our family. Now we spend nights worrying for our addict's safety, we spend time crying as we imagine what it is like for our addict to sit in a jail cell, or we grope for strength to find the right words to explain to our children what happened to our failed marriage. From our standpoint, we fight a losing battle with guilt on all fronts.

Enabling is a strong factor in the picture of guilt. Yet, there are other contributors in this blame game. Guilt held us captive when we continued to cling to the false notion that we could have done something to prevent this disease. We now know that we cannot fix or control the disease of addiction and that we did not cause this disease, but do give ourselves credit for trying. We exerted enormous amounts of time and energy in our futile efforts to fix and control our addict. No wonder we live with guilt! We tried to play God, and we are surprised that we failed miserably. We got a wake-up call, a rude awakening on the day we discovered that all of our loving, enabling, addictive attempts got us nowhere (and in some cases, plunged our addict into even greater depths of addiction). Guilt gnawed away at our sanity as we considered time wasted and efforts expended—all for naught. We meant well, but we were in over our heads, weren't we? So alongside our guilt of enabling, we now add the burden of the guilt we carry in our role as attempted (but failed) fixers.

If we hope to discover any peace and resolution from the baggage of guilt we now carry around with us, we must examine yet another aspect of blame in our family guilt trip. We are committed to leaving no stone unturned in this trip; our journey requires forthright honesty if we hope to rid our families of the millstone of guilt that is weighing us down.

Over and over again, guilt ruled with its strong upper hand as we stood by and harshly reprimanded ourselves for our inability to follow through on our threats and demands. One moment, we told our addict that he would not be allowed in our house with alcohol, but the next moment, we were tucking him into bed and pouring out his remaining liquor. In a strong moment of decision, we put our collective feet down, telling our addict she could not bring drugs into our home, but later, we gave in to her constant begging. We handed her money, knowing full well the cash would end up in the drug dealer's hands. One night, after a beating, we promised our children we would escape to the safety of a shelter, but the morning after, we concealed our bruises underneath our clothing.

Some of us live with the guilt of past remembrances. Thinking back into our childhood, we recalled that time in school when we almost broke down and confided in our teacher. Instead, we went home to addiction. We put our addicted parent to bed and prepared dinner for our siblings. Now the guilt of the past and the present haunt us. We belittle ourselves for our lack of courage. We chastise ourselves for our inability to move forward with firm steps leading to decisive action. We ridicule ourselves for our gullibility, our naïveté, and our vulnerability.

None of us could fathom how smart the disease of addiction turned out to be or how easily we allowed our addict to outsmart us. We stand back, amazed, when our addict used the gifts of persuasion. Family members carry guilt from what we assess as our stupidity, but let us never forget just how deviously this disease works and how quickly it twists our addict into an unrecognizable person. Addicts possess universal characteristics, none of which we have found to be particularly charming. The disease causes them to be self-centered. They can lie to us, manipulate us, and worry us to the point that we live in constant fear of their well-being. We worry whether this disease will eventually kill our family member.

Most addicts are not mean, vicious, or conniving people, but they quickly become that way when they are captured by the influence of the drug of their choice. The disease of addiction quickly sapped our loved one of his or her ability to make wise choices. His or her personality, appearance, physical health, and moral conscience changed rapidly once addiction took its hold upon our addict's life. One day we woke up and wondered who this stranger in our household was. We mourned the loss of an individual who had great potential and wonderful gifts. This potential and these gifts are wasted away from the affects of addiction.

Our child, who used to be the straight-A student, cannot even manage to get to class. Our spouse, whose steady job made us so proud, now spends the paycheck on feeding his or her addictive habit. The parent who used to make our school lunch can now barely get out of the bed to wish us goodbye. We still love these people, but we hate their disease. We also hate what this disease does to our families, because we become so wrapped up in the addict's problems that they become our own. We are *addicted* to the addict. We are filled with guilt because we see no means of escape from the control this disease has on our family.

In the early stages of addiction, our addict was in denial, and we might also be trapped into denial as well. All the signs may be present as we began to notice changes in the lifestyle of our addicts. We denied the signs, thinking, *Surely we must be mistaken.* As we become more and more aware of the signs, we may overlook their significance. Maybe our daughter now wears long sleeves, even in extremely hot weather, yet we kept telling ourselves nothing is unusual. "Surely she is not hiding a drug problem," we say. Denial allows addicts to continue to avoid facing their substance abuse. Denial also enables family members to avoid confronting the problems of addiction.

Addiction is a progressive disease. The disease always gets worse until the addict and family members are willing to get help. By denying the seriousness of the problem, we joined our addicts in pretending things were not as bad as they seemed. We mistakenly thought that somewhere out there, an acceptable *level* of addiction existed.

We also denied how damaging the effects of addiction are on our family's health and well-being. Addiction may be bluntly characterized as a selfish disease. Our addict rationalized and justified the truth of his or her lies. The addict sought self-gratification at all times. He or she easily justified trampling over our property, boundaries, and emotions to serve his or her needs. We have allowed ourselves to be manipulated, lied to, and taken advantage of over and over again, often with the mistaken belief that we were helping our addict. We overlooked our addict's thefts and dishonesty, particularly in the early stages of addiction. Because we wanted peace in the family, we chose to ignore the problem rather than confront the addict. We placated the addict to avoid conflict. We tried to convince ourselves that our addict was telling the truth. In our hearts, we knew better, so we pushed aside the voice of conscience and morality. We now burn with guilt and are filled with shame because we can no longer deny what should have been so obvious. We have an addict in our family, and we are as addicted as our addict is.

Eventually families come to the point where denial plays an invalid role in our family life. The progression of the disease makes it impossible to ignore and sweep addiction under the rug. Unfortunately, once the veil of denial is lifted away to reveal the depth of the addiction, our preoccupation as a family has often grown into a full-blown obsession. We constantly worry about our addict, and our life becomes centered on him or her. My husband and I became so obsessed with our loved one that I must admit that our mood often depended on how well *he* was doing. Our addict's addiction became the biggest and most important issue in our world. His addiction dominated our lives. We thought about it day and night. Our obsession grew stronger and stronger as our loved one's disease progressed.

My husband and I would go out for a relaxing, romantic dinner, and our addict would call just as we were seated in a restaurant. We might be relaxed, quietly talking after a hard workday, and suddenly our mood would change, depending on the conversation with our loved one. If he was in a good mood, so were we. If he was having a bad day, our mood suddenly changed. Our dinner conversation shifted to center on him. This was not the fault of our addict. We in no way blamed him for intruding into our lives. We welcomed his conversation and were glad he had called. Yet, we were so obsessed with our addict that his phone call had the power to determine our frame of mind! For this reason, we became as sick as our addict. Looking back, both my husband and I were guilty of letting our addict overshadow our lives, but we seemed to have no ability to not let this disease dominate even our dinner plans.

Family members can easily lose their own sense of personal identity. Our lives are put on hold while we deal with the issues of addiction. Our state of living is determined by what is happening in the lives of our addict rather than in our own lives.

Shame and guilt often resulted in attempts to cover up what was happening in our family life. We lived with our secrets, afraid to reveal them to outsiders. If we confided in others, our family members might become the scapegoats for our addict. We learned quickly that many people have little background in understanding or comprehending the disease of addiction. Some of these people are more than ready to point out our family failures and weaknesses and declare us guilty. We are charged and convicted as partners with our addict in causing the addiction. Others listened patiently and with sympathy, but from their blank stares, we knew they did not have a clue. On very rare occasions, we found acquaintances who truly empathized with us, some of whom have walked in our addiction shoes, but these people were few and far between. When we found these individuals, we latched on to them, lapping up their attention.

Since addiction reigned over our lives, our stories of addiction prevailed in our conversation with others. In many instances, we spent so much time talking about our problems that our conversations lacked any substance but substance abuse. The inevitable result was that our co-workers and friends grew weary of our conversations. They avoided us, knowing that they were only in for a litany of our recent addiction stories. Most of them sounded too horrible or unrealistic to be true anyway. Some onlookers thought our insanity has driven us to make up these bizarre tales. We were listened to with amusement or pity, for our stories appeared to some to be pure fantasies.

Those who understood were few, so when we found these people, we tended to overcompensate for others' lack of perception. We showered these people with story after story. After a while, we discovered that even these friends began to avoid us because our addiction stories overshadowed any social event. Even in the presence of inquiring friends, my husband and I have learned over time to limit our stories. We sometimes forget that simply because addiction has dominated and ruled *our* lives, it does not dominate and rule the lives of others. Our family reacted by testing the waters of others' reactions before stepping in too far and overwhelming people. With some individuals, we have found that we can share limited amounts of information, but with others, we can be much more open.

Consider the dilemma we faced in our guilt game: when we overstepped our boundaries, we quickly withdrew. We tried not to offend others or bombard them with too much information. In our minds, we thought we made fools of ourselves by sharing too much or by burdening others with our incessant stories; therefore, we were filled with guilt. Yet, when we concealed our secrets (even out of respect for others), we were plagued with the guilt of secrecy. We concluded that our best solution was to keep our problems within the walls of our family, even if that cover-up added stress to family life. Over time, we tended to draw inward into our family life and keep quiet. We reasoned that covering up our family secrets was surely better than having people whisper behind our backs or look at us like we had lost our minds.

Yet as people of faith, surely we can share openly and honestly with our pastor and fellow church members, right? We learned to not assume that our ministers or our church friends will understand. We will be truly blessed if we can find a minister who has a background in addiction. Many do not; as such, they will have no understanding of what we are talking about. Hopefully, they will listen sympathetically to our stories, pray with us, and offer us advice. Unfortunately, it has been my experience that most pastors lack training or experience to cope with families of addicts. Some may offer poor advice, so proceed cautiously. Being a pastor myself, I have strived to show great sensitivity in guiding families of addicts. Many come to me carrying heavy loads of guilt. In some cases, family members carry the guilt of having to admit their addiction story to their pastor, hoping they will not be judged harshly in the process.

Just as we came to understand that pastors rarely understand this disease, we also learned not to assume that our fellow church members held much knowledge either. Think back to a time when we knew nothing or very little about the disease of addiction. We must put ourselves in the shoes of others and realize their positions. Many of them are caring people who simply cannot begin to rationalize or comprehend what we are sharing with them. Others will be judgmental and critical of our families. The stark reality is that people of faith—the very people we worship with each Sunday—may or may not be sources of help and care for your family. Because we were blindsided by their actions, our family was left speechless and overwhelmed with guilt.

The domination of this disease greatly impacted the dynamics of family life. The disease profoundly affected our relationship with other family members. Remember that addiction forced us to focus on one person: the addict. Caring for our addict monopolized our every waking moment. Shunned family members vied for our attention, but we were too busy with our addict. Now faced with the harsh truth of our neglect, we realize there were others who needed our time and effort as much as our addict. Over the years, these ignored family members begin to express resentments. Neglected family members lashed out with angry words. Pent-up emotions built up to the boiling point. Things may have gotten so out of hand that we are now alienated from some of these family members. We are left with severed or at least damaged relationships. We wonder if the damage we have done is beyond repair. Many of us are taking necessary steps toward mending these relationships, but we know healing takes a great deal of time and effort. Even as we work toward restored relationships, we are annoyed by guilt.

Negative thoughts and guilt feelings are inevitable in families of addicts. We have firsthand experience with negativity and guilt. We all need to learn how to rid ourselves of the unhealthy guilt we showered upon ourselves. Now is the time to heal from the self-imposed and other-imposed guilt. God desires us to be whole people, not people who constantly live with the guilt of past mistakes.

We serve a God of forgiveness who time and again in biblical history forgave the mistakes of His children. Think about David, who became Israel's greatest king. He made the mistake of entering into an adulterous relationship with Bathsheba. Then, in his jealously, he had her husband murdered. God forgave David, but David had the choice of accepting or rejecting God's forgiveness. David chose forgiveness and thus was enabled to answer the call of God to assume great leadership. David found he could not continue to wallow in the miserable pit of guilt and faithfully serve God at the same time. Neither can we. Getting rid of guilt takes time; it does not happen overnight. Many of the psalms in the Bible are attributed to David. When we read these psalms, we do not encounter the strong King David as much as we do the fragile, human David who struggled with his infirmities of guilt.

I would suggest that we commit as a family to reading together one psalm of David each day. As we do so, our family will learn a necessary but freeing lesson about alleviating guilt. Through the lens of the psalms, we will clearly view David's guilt and see that this guilt was not instantly removed. In psalm after psalm, David cried out to God for forgiveness from the pain of guilt. David received God's forgiveness, but needed time to reflect and comprehend the gift God offered him. How we wish we could snap our fingers and have guilt removed from our family life. Cleaning our family life of all the grime and filth of guilt takes the ingredients of time, grace, love, and the acceptance of God's forgiveness. We must not be ashamed to turn to God for help. We must earnestly believe that God offers our family forgiveness and that only God can clean away the guilt from our addiction choices.

The psalmist humbly pleaded to God:

> *"For your name's sake, O Lord, pardon my guilt,*
> *for it is great."*
>
> *Psalms 25:11 (NRSV)*

In the simplicity of this verse of Scripture, we are presented a true, straightforward picture of guilt. The psalmist, in an almost unnoticeable way, described the depths of guilt. There is a mighty significance in what the psalmist is revealing in the phrase, *"for it is great."* We could hurriedly read these words and miss the truth behind the words. The words are placed in the psalms in such an unobtrusive manner that we could easily skip over them. The words convey to us that the psalmist experienced *great* guilt. The psalmist confessed that he possessed no ordinary guilt. Furthermore, the psalmist challenged God to prove His very nature and His very name when associated with this great guilt. The psalmist fervently believed that forgiveness and pardon were a part of the very essence of God's being and were tied up in His willingness to pardon and forgive such consuming guilt. God's name was on the line, so to speak. What the psalmist believed about God and what the psalms had been taught about God would be nullified if He were unable to pardon guilt of this magnitude. The very nature of God rested on His removal of guilt. The psalmist issued the challenge to God, confident that He would come through! God's actions of forgiveness not only vindicated His name and His nature, but also truly revealed the majesty and power of God.

Like the psalmist, as families of addicts, we admit that our guilt is not petty and small. Like the psalmist, we too conceal great guilt. Naming and claiming our guilt before God pushes our family on the road to recovery and further and further away from the clutches of guilt. Trusting that God and God alone washes away and erases the marks of guilt upon our family moves us forward on the path toward freedom. Begin as a family to share with one another the guilt the family harbors. Bring this guilt before God.

> *"Then I acknowledged my sin to you, and I did not hide my iniquity; I said, "I will confess my transgressions to the Lord', and you forgave the guilt of my sin."*
>
> *Psalms 32:5 (NRSV)*

We need to confess to God (and to one another) the guilt that has been eating away at our souls. Be totally honest. We should freely share our hurts with one another and listen with sensitive ears and a compassionate heart when family members proclaim their benedictions of guilt. Do not play the blame game. Enough blame and guilt has rested on the shoulders of our family members already. Guilt and blame have shackled us to our fears and doubts. It is time to let God set us free. We are dearly beloved children of God. Approach Him as a child, for our Parent God's arms will be outstretched, waiting for us. Come in faith and trust. Accept God's forgiveness as a precious gift. Bask in the light of God's forgiveness.

We also need to understand that the eradication of guilt may take a lifetime. In the days ahead, guilt will lift up its ugly head from time to time. Some family members may refuse to acknowledge or accept God's forgiveness as they continue along the path of resentment and the road of guilt. On a bad day, when hopelessness reigns, when we anticipate no avenue of release for our addicts, guilt will rear up and kick us right in the face. Grounding ourselves in God's love, mercy, grace, and forgiveness is necessary. We find comfort when we turn to the Scriptures, especially the book of Psalms. I would advise family members to select devotional readings that reiterate God's forgiveness from guilt. Offer earnest prayers to God. Engage in conversations with a trusted friend or family member. Seek professional or pastoral help as needed. These mighty tools will fortify our faith and surround us like walls of protection.

Our acceptance of God's forgiveness has nothing whatsoever to do with whether our addicts work programs of recovery or not. Our families, with God's sustaining help, must work their own programs of forgiveness. Like a ball and chain, addiction kept us prisoners to guilt. Addiction gladly hoarded the key, locking us in our own cells of despair and shame. Our guilt revolved around our addict, imprisoning us into thinking that our addict's recovery was the only means for us to be set free. Do not buy into this nonsense. God alone holds the key. Our release from the stronghold of addiction is not dependent on our addicts.

Hear this message loudly and clearly, and hear it as a scream of relief: God and God alone holds the key of forgiveness for our families and for us. For too long, our existence, our measure of security, our sense of happiness, and our expectation of any glimpse of hope fell squarely on the shoulders of our addict. We must release him or her from this unrealistic expectation and this unreasonable burden. As ridiculous as this may sound, we anchored our forgiveness on the one person whose boat of life was violently caught in the storm of addiction. Unfairly and unjustly, we turned our security of forgiveness over to the one person who was so far from the safe shore of life that he could not possibly find an anchor to toss us. We were left drowning in the sea of guilt with no lifeline to save us.

Finding a secure anchor does not save us. Only the anchor of our faith in God can ultimately guide us to the shores of forgiveness. God's lighthouse of forgiveness guides us safely to the harbor of peace. The storms of life will require us to put down anchors all along the journey. We offer the gift of forgiveness for ourselves by allowing God to wash us clean of guilt and actually accepting God's forgiveness. We extend the circle of forgiveness for others when we seek to make amends for both our wrongs and their wrongs. We reach out with forgiveness for our addict when we do not condone his or her addiction, but do offer grace to our lost child, spouse, or parent. Guilt allows us no permission to forgive either others or ourselves. God's forgiveness empowers us to do both.

There are strings attached to forgiveness. "What?" you say. "Forgiveness is not unconditional?" While God's love and grace are unconditional, forgiveness drives a hard bargain. Just when we thought we could selfishly grab God's forgiveness and be about our own business, the gospel of Matthew shatters our naïve thinking and our immature faith. Jesus speaks with authority:

> *"For if you forgive other their trespasses, your heavenly Father will also forgive you; but if you do not forgive others, neither will your Father forgive your trespasses."*
>
> *Matthew 6:14–15 (NRSV)*

Great! Just when we thought we could get off the hook, Jesus presents us with a hard lesson. Does Jesus mean we must extend forgiveness to family members who have offended us, to those friends who have slandered us, or even to our addict who has belittled us? "Come on, Jesus. Have we not suffered enough already?" you might say. "Have we not paid the price? Surely, families of addicts are exempt from this command, are we not?" Among all the lessons we learn as students in our school of addiction, perhaps this one may be the most difficult. Yet, this is a lesson we must be taught, a truth we must comprehend, and a commandment we must fulfill in order for us to gain freedom from the addiction of guilt.

Here is another ironic and puzzling lesson to learn in the game of addiction.

Just when we thought our cards in life dealt us the winning hand of God's forgiveness, we encounter the trump card. God's forgiveness cannot fully take root, sprout, and grow to full fruition in our lives unless we sow the seeds of our forgiveness into the lives of others. In the saying, "blessed to be a blessing," we get the circular effect of blessing. God blesses us so we can bless others, and in turn, we receive a blessing. Jesus adds a similar dimension to the concept of God's forgiveness. We are "forgiven to be forgiving." Jesus knew that God's healing powers of forgiveness could never fully work in our lives until we forgive others. Like the circle of blessing, Jesus offers a circle of forgiveness. We are forgiven, so we forgive others, and then we experience the full power of forgiveness. Imagine the results of God's forgiveness in our lives if we extend forgiveness to those we declare guilty and responsible for our guilt. Think of all the ways God's forgiveness would lift the pain of guilt from our lives when we practice forgiving others.

We will never reach a level of maturity in our walk with God or in our walk toward recovery until we learn to accept God's forgiveness and offer forgiveness to others. Both are essential steps in our faith journey and our recovery journey. A good way to begin is by offering forgiveness to those in our own family circles. A necessary step is to ask them to forgive us for our wrongs. We may have to reach out in reconciliation to some family members who were neglected as we centered on the needs and problems of our addicts. Reach out to these family members. Realize that those shunned by our lack of attention need time to rebuild their trust in us. We can never make up for lost time, but we can begin to restore and rebuild these fragile relationships.

Just as we plead with people to forgive us, we must also reach out with the hand of forgiveness. The unappreciated and intrusive criticism of family members is not easily forgotten, but it can be forgiven. The failed support of friends, the gossip of uninformed neighbors, and the piety of our church acquaintances are all situations to cast aside in the name of forgiveness. Living with grudges only harms us. Living with past mistakes only stresses us. Forgiveness frees us to claim our birthright as children of God, who are created in God's image and for whom God ordains for a purpose-driven future.

Now we come to the one person who some of us think deserves little or no forgiveness: the addict. Some of us may discover that the most difficult person to forgive is this very loved one who destroyed our lives. Others of us may find it easier to forgive our addict than ourselves. Whichever case fits us, our addicts yearn for our forgiveness and our unconditional love. Some addicts may carry around enormous amounts of guilt for their actions. Addicts in a program of recovery are often instructed to make amends for their destructive behaviors. When our addicts come to us to make amends, we must not turn our backs on them. Listen carefully and patiently. Do not exhibit an "I-told-you-so" attitude. Our addicts already have enough guilt without our heaping on more. Making amends is no easy task for them. Addicts live with guilt day in and day out. Our support—not our sarcasm—will speak volumes to our addicts. Our forgiveness—not our condemnation—will have a lasting impact on our addict's recovery.

Forgiveness ranks at the top as one of the key elements of healing. Anger and guilt diminish our capacity to fully experience God's goodness. Strong relationships are built on forgiveness. Never underestimate the strength of forgiveness to turn lives around and rebuild fractured relationships. The writer of Psalm 32 says, in verse 5, *"Then, I acknowledged my sin to you, and I did not hide my iniquity."* Addiction is not a sin; it is a disease. Our sin stems from continuing to live with our guilt and letting this guilt eat away at our dignity. Our sin comes from believing that we are marked unworthy by God and stamped as "guilty" for the rest of our lives. Our sin flows from our unwillingness to forgive. The good news awaits us. In our confession before Almighty God, we are granted forgiveness, and the good news becomes a reality in our everyday living.

Addiction caught us as prey in the trap of guilt. Like a frightened animal, we knew no escape. Then, just when we thought we were trapped forever, God's unconditional love sprang open the hinges and set us free. Our forgiveness of others and ourselves gave us the strength to escape. Even in the midst of addiction, we refused to be captive to guilt ever again.

So, come and bring your guilt offerings to God. Lay them on the altar of God's forgiveness. Our offerings will be found acceptable to God. Our offerings will be more than sufficient to meet the requirements for atonement. The aroma of our sacrifices will be pleasing to God. Smell the sweet fragrance of God's forgiveness as our guilt is burned away on the altar of God's love. As we inhale, let us breathe out the poisonous smoke of guilt and breathe in the fresh wind of forgiveness.

CHAPTER THREE:

How Does Addiction Impact My Christian Life?

"Now when Job's three friends heard of all these troubles that had come upon him, each of them set out from his home—Eliphaz the Temanite, Bildad the Shuhite, and Zophar the Naamathite. They met together to go and console and comfort him. When they saw him from a distance, they did not recognize him, and they raised their voices and wept aloud; they tore their robes and threw dust into the air upon their heads. They sat with him on the ground for seven days and seven nights, and no one spoke a word to him, for they saw that his suffering was very great."

Job 2:11–13 (NRSV)

From reading the story of righteous, suffering Job, some of us have concluded that if Job had the kind of friends depicted in the biblical book, then who needs enemies? Job's friends vehemently defend the commonly held theology of the day that God rewarded good and punished evil. So, they never wavered from their belief that Job's sins caused God to inflict such devastating punishment upon him. Let us give Job's friends credit for at least one admirable quality, however: they, at least, *showed up.* They wept with Job, mourned with Job, and sat with Job, day and night, until he was able to share with them his horrifying story. That's more than we can say for some of our friends, is it not?

When some families were thrust into the fury of addiction, they could boast that some of their friends never, not for one moment, criticized them, never once blamed them, or it never occurred to them to heap guilt upon their backs as Job's friends did. The harsh, bitter, sad reality for other families of addicts is that some of their friends never showed up at all; they ignored these families altogether. Job was given the opportunity to do something they were not. At least he was allowed to try to defend himself against the friends' accusations. These neglected families yearned for friends in whom to confide, sought out friends to share their pain, but some friends always seemed too busy to listen or too quick to judge. Individuals simply could not believe these families were afflicted in such a devastating manner.

Many of these families are people of faith. They worship every Sunday in the pew near some of their accusers. Their families, from all outward appearances, seemed to them to be nice and respectable people. These friends often feel as if these families of addicts fooled them. These friends' lack of understanding about addiction or their believing that these families were to blame caused some people to shun them and point a finger of guilt at the family members. They were written off as complete failures because they could not control their addicts. Maybe, like Job's friends, they reasoned that they must have done something to deserve their punishment. So these families were left alone, abandoned by those they thought they could rely upon when times got tough.

Some of these very people who never gave these families a chance to tell their side of the story were friends in their own circles of faith. Some families of addicts were amazed that those who professed the merits of forgiveness, grace, and love would not give them the time of day. They sat in Sunday school classes with individuals who talked of reaching out to others in need, but then these same people turned their backs on these families in a time of need. Some had the audacity to tell them if they had prayed hard enough or had enough faith, this would not have happened to their loved ones in the first place. Since the addict's family obviously lacked faith, then associating with them would taint their accusers. It's better to leave them alone to drown in the pool of their own deserved punishment. Once the fires of gossip were fueled among their network of acquaintances (and even in their own congregations of faith), there was no stopping some from finding them guilty without having first given the benefit of the doubt. They were written off, characterized as "that family with the addict." Belittled, they were left alone to solve their problems with little spiritual guidance.

Some of these friends were loyal for a while—until the addicted families began to wear on their nerves. That time came when, rightly or wrongly, these families were perceived as bringing a measure of insanity into others' calm lives. For some, it was too much. Families of addicts shook apart their values of right and wrong, leaving them with only shades of gray. These families shattered their friends' peaceful and tranquil lives with their addiction stories. Families with addicts spoke the truth, thinking it would set them free, but their friends would have preferred half-truths because the truth was far too unsettling, way too frightening, and seemed absurd.

Perhaps some of these friends quickly learned how to steer the subject away from addiction and on to more pleasant matters. Maybe invitations to social gatherings dwindled, friends stopping calling, and these families were left to their own demise. Or maybe their friends were embarrassed for them, afraid they might spoil their dinners with their constant babbling about their latest addiction crisis, so they were left out of the social circles where they once traveled. Addiction put these families at the mercy of others.

Families of addicts sometimes unknowingly overstep their bounds, saying and doing the wrong things, thus upsetting friends who prayed these families' horror stories did not ever play out in their lives. These families became risky commodities and some people wished to avoid contact with them. They did not exactly fit the description of "life of the party," did they? They were not the individuals who lifted up the spirits of their friends over coffee.

These families of addicts considered themselves truly blessed to find some friends who listened patiently to their stories, cried with them, prayed with them, and offered them unconditional love. They were there in the darkest hours. Perhaps these friends were few and far between. They may have encountered some people who were good friends to the family, but deep inside, their families knew their acquaintances could not quite comprehend their true emotions or show real empathy; they did not share the same experiences of addiction. Yet, they thanked God for these friends, who in spite of not quite knowing what to do or say, refused to let go of their hands. They could ascertain from their faces that their stories were unbelievable but were never really questioned. They could gather from their demeanor that their experiences shocked these friends with the blunt reality of the burdens the family carried, but these friends never abandoned the addicted family. These families sometimes took advantage of the friendship of these particular friends, clinging to the sincere acts of friendship as a means of survival.

Some of these friends acted and thought exactly like Job's friends. They questioned the motives of these families, they offered simple and pious solutions to their problems, and they challenged the family member's theological thinking. These friends, like the friends of Job, may have reflected poor theology, but they were faithful and sincere. They stuck with these families through thick and thin, even if their theology of suffering was warped and needed fine tuning. Some friends, like Job's friends, may have expressed the sentiment that somehow these families were responsible for the family addiction. They forced these addicted families to get their theology of suffering in order, and they stretched them to seek an alternative viewpoint. The book of Job was written to challenge the dominant thinking of the day about suffering. The belief was that the sufferer was a sinner and thus deserved his or her due punishment. Job radically refuted this idea, assuring us that he was a righteous man who had done absolutely nothing to deserve the circumstances he endured.

Hopefully, those families in these situations are able to convince their friends, who acted liked Job's friends that addiction stems from a disease, not from sin. Families in these cases should not be too hard on their friends, however. At least these friends were there for them when others abandoned the family. Not everyone whom the families of addicts encounter will have a mature theology about the disease of addiction. Like Job's friends, these friends can be thanked for pushing them to explore the avenues of suffering and arrive at a mature, solid theological understanding. Their responsibility in acquiring such a theology is to share it with others who lack such knowledge.

This theology affirms that we serve a God who does not cause suffering, but who walks with us through suffering, giving us the strength to endure. Our theology places no blame on our addict or us. Instead of criticizing these friends for their shallow theology, families in these situations can be thankful for the steadfast loyalty of their friends. Family members should work diligently to correct misguided theological viewpoints they encounter when dealing with friends, church members, or acquaintances.

Often, such families found they could only truly open up to groups of friends who had walked the journey of addiction. Only in a support group of other families who knew the tribulations they encountered could these families let down their guard and be totally comfortable. Only by talking and sharing with other families experienced in addiction could they be totally honest. This is why it is vitally important to seek out other families, particularly families of faith, who can truly empathize with families of addicts.

For some families of addicts, the above scenarios never played out on any stage. They decided, from the very beginning, to keep their family addiction quiet. They hid the secrets behind the closed doors of family life. Their silence was costly; it required these families to be constantly on guard around co-workers, friends, and church members. To them, though, it was worth the secrecy to avoid the pain and criticism of others. They stretched the truth about what was really happening in their family life. They covered up for their addicts and made excuse after excuse. They plastered on a fake smile when their hearts were broken. They avoided the eye contact of their co-workers who seemed reluctant to buy into the pretense of why they are always late or missing work.

Keeping quiet about family addiction has taken its toll on them, however. Their emotions continually run the gamut from panic, anxiety, relief, doubt, and hope. These families have no one to confide in about their situation (and would probably not trust an outsider anyway). They live with the fear of being discovered; yet, ironically, they would breathe a sigh of relief if they could get everything out in the open. Their family has been drained of emotion, stressed beyond the breaking point, and depressed to the point of needing medical and spiritual help. They are worn out from the many burdens of deception. Addiction has worked them like a slave driver, never giving them a break, and dominating their family life, day in and day out. Who would even begin to understand their bizarre stories anyway? *It's best to keep silent,* they reason. Addiction has driven them into holes of seclusion that have turned out to be anything but hiding places of security, and nothing and no one can pry them out.

Perhaps some families of addicts easily find themselves in the some of these scenarios. However, others' families may relate better to the experience of my family. We were blessed to have caring friends, especially in our faith community, who did not judge our family. Instead, they offered support and friendship. I thank God every day for these friends and acquaintances who listened carefully and who continue, to this day, to offer prayers for my addict and for our family.

However, whatever situation we may find ourselves in, all families of addicts recognize that given the selfish nature of the disease, our relationship with God and with others is at times strained. We are so centered on our addicts that we often neglect our friends and fail to strengthen our relationship with others. We realize that even the most faithful of our friends cannot fully understand what we face unless they experience addiction in their family life.

Whatever our relationship with friends and acquaintances, we honestly admit that addiction not only affects our relationships with others but with God as well. We may religiously continue our regular practices of worship and faithful attendance at the events of our communities of faith. In spite of this, many of us find ourselves drained spiritually, only going through the motions of worship and praise without much sincerity. Addiction invades our spiritual life, depletes our spiritual resources, and leaves us as penitent worshippers. Do we not identify with the Old Testament prophet Ezekiel and his valley of dry bones? God brought Ezekiel to a valley of dry bones and plopped him down right in the middle. A valley of dry bones perfectly depicts our spiritual lives, does it not?

> *"The hand of the Lord came upon me, and he brought me out by the spirit of the Lord and set me down in the middle of a valley; it was full of bones. He led me all round them; there were many lying in the valley, and they were very dry. He said to me, 'Mortal, can these bones live?' I answered 'O Lord God, you know.' Then he said to me, 'Prophesy to these bones and say to them: O dry bones, hear the word of the Lord.' Thus says the Lord God to these bones: I will cause breath to enter you, and you shall live."*
>
> *Ezekiel 37:1–5 (NRSV)*

Dealing with addiction can drain the joy out of our spiritual lives. At times, our prayers contain shallow words of pleading, our hymns of praise are sung in a lackluster fashion, our Scripture readings are devoid of joy, and Sunday sermons miss the mark. We are tempted to blame God, but we know spiritual dryness goes along with the territory of addiction. We have become dry bones in the valley of addiction. Like Ezekiel, God asks us, "Mortal, can these bones live?" Given the chasm we must breach to restore our faith, we can only reply with the exact words of the prophet: "O Lord God, you know." We search for answers about faith and come up short. We wait and wait, knowing that only God could bring the dry bones of our faith back to life, but wondering when the miracle would happen. When would God breathe into our dry spiritual bones the breath of life so that we could worship again with fervor? When would God restore the joy of our salvation? Like the psalmist, we cry out: *"Restore to me the joy of your salvation and sustain in me a willing spirit"* (Psalms 51:12 (NRSV)).

How does addiction impact our spiritual lives? The question has a two-sided dimension, focusing upon both our relationship with God and our relationships with others. These two relationships are bound together and cannot be separated when we consider how addiction impacts our spiritual lives. When He was questioned about what He perceived was the greatest commandment, Jesus tied the two intricately together. Jesus answered that the commandment anchored on one's complete love of God and one's full love of neighbor as exemplified in our own love of self. To allow God to breathe new life into our dry spiritual bones, we must examine our relationship with others and our relationship with God. Honestly probing into the details of both relationships are not meant to pry. Rather, honestly examining our heart and lives confronts those barriers we have erected that prevent the spirit of God from breathing new life into our dry bones. Let us hear afresh the words of Jesus as He linked together the spiritual dimension of loving God and neighbor:

> *"One of the scribes came near and hearing them disputing with one another, and seeing that he answered them well, he asked him, 'Which commandment is the first of all?' Jesus answered, 'The first is 'Hear, O Israel: The Lord our God, the Lord is one; you shall love the Lord your God with all you heart, and with all your soul, and with all your mind, and with all your strength.' The second is this, 'You shall love your neighbor as yourself.' "There is no other commandment greater than these."*
>
> *Mark 12:28–31 (NRSV)*

Before we go any further in our discussion, let us take time to dwell on these words of Jesus. I would invite us to sit down for a few relaxing moments of peace and reflection. This is a time to quiet our hearts and our bodies and remove any distractions. Take a piece of paper and write on one column **Relationship with God** and on another column **Relationship with Others.** Write under each column key words or phrases that describe your relationship with God and relationships with others. Put down under the section **Relationship with God** the ways we are hindered in our ability to worship and serve God. Include names of friends, family members, and church members under **Relationship with Others**. By each name, indicate whether this person offered the family love and support or just the opposite. Write down any positive or negative feelings toward these people. As families share together thoughts on how addiction has affected their faith, it is helpful to keep this list visible. This list will help us identify dry areas in our spiritual walks with God as well as naming people who have helped or hindered us in the addiction journey.

Each of us caught in the addiction drama face the dilemma of knowing what to share, when to share, how much to share, and with whom to share our addiction story.

One of the questions we encounter is simply who can we trust? Who can we depend upon to be trustworthy? These questions derive from our trust in God. We serve God, who is trustworthy. We expect people who have entered into a covenant relationship with God to be trustworthy as well. We come away disappointed when people we confided in broke the relationship of trust, especially fellow church members who professed faith in God. We must never let our trust in God be dependent upon how other believers react. Even well-meaning people of faith will let us down and violate our trust. Do not let the lack of trust on the part of fellow believers keep us from trusting in God.

Each day is a learning process in the journey of addiction. Over time, we will know the people we can trust. The more we travel the addiction road, the wiser and more discerning we will become. We must not be too hard on ourselves for blunders we have made in the past where we shared too much and our trust was violated. Remember that each situation is unique. There are times when we sense we need to share large amounts of information. At other times, we may proceed with caution. Ask God to grant each family member the wisdom to discern the people who are trustworthy and the people who are ready to receive our addiction stories. We will be amazed at the ways God will bring people into our lives whose families are also struggling with addiction issues.

Learning to forgive others and ourselves is important. When we blurt out more information than people are able to process, we should not get down on ourselves. Understand that some people are not able to accept what we are telling them. When we share information we trusted people to keep in confidence, only to find it emerging as the latest gossip tabloid in our friends' grapevines, we learn to forgive people and proceed with caution the next time. Each family must determine when they are ready to share with others. No family has the obligation to share any more than they wish. Only the family members understand the dynamics at work in each individual's family life. Our family decides when, where, and with whom to share the family story. Do not feel pressure to tell this story until the family members are ready. Plunged into the depths of addiction, we need time to process what is happening to our families.

My husband and I made the decision to be very open about our addiction story, but this decision evolved over time. We proceeded at first with caution. We were selective in our initial process of sharing. We started with some people we knew we could trust. In my case, it was the staff with whom I worked at my church. In my husband's case, it was some co-workers and close friends. The more we moved into this addiction journey, the further we were able to open up. Now we are committed to sharing our story very openly and freely. We earnestly believe that God places people within our lives who need to hear our story and to be strengthened by our message of hope.

One morning, as I was leaving a business that I rarely frequented, a church member flagged me down. I had forgotten my parishioner worked at this establishment. She requested prayer for a family member dealing with addiction. She felt compelled to talk rapidly and incessantly to try to justify and rationalize the actions of the loved one, thinking I would have little knowledge of the subject without her explanation. Her demeanor totally changed when I stopped her and assured her I fully related to her chaotic situation. A calming presence came over her as she realized that we had a bond together as fellow family members of addicts. As one of her pastors, she knew I would honor her prayer request and keep her story in the strictest confidence. Yet, she came away from our conversation also knowing that she had my additional support and understanding that only the family member of an addict could offer. Our conversation granted her freedom to talk with me openly without my judging her family or her.

Since we made the decision to share honestly about our family situation, my husband and I have been awed and amazed at the times in which God has placed people in our lives in unique ways. Often, out of the blue, when we least expect it, a person shocks us by disclosing that his or her family contains an addict. Sometimes an offhanded remark from an individual leads us to probe deeper. Sometimes a comment we make inspires another person to engage us in conversation. The families of ministers are often placed on a pedestal. We are viewed through rose-colored glasses and held to unrealistic expectations. If nothing else, our sharing has shattered the unrealistic illusion of perfection that others place around clergy families.

Our addict was dealt with the double blow of a dual diagnosis, a determination that the addiction was complicated by other medical conditions. Thus, he tried a myriad of different treatment options and had been in numerous recovery centers. God has opened up numerous doors of opportunity for us to share with addictive families about paths toward recovery. We cherish this responsibility as a sacred trust from God. We have bookmarked on our computer Web sites where families can search for good, quality recovery centers, some of which offer specialized treatment. We are honored when people seek our advice, but furthermore, we sensed a call from God to help others in the area of addiction. Our efforts would have never come to fruition if we had been unwilling to share.

My husband and I are compelled and called by God to share. Does this mean we are always successful in our efforts? We have as many failures as successes, due to the nature of addiction. Some people are not ready to hear what we tell them. They have not been in the journey of addiction long enough to believe that what we say to them might actually happen. The stark yet realistic picture we paint for them seems too harsh and unbelievable. Some do not want to accept the consequences or the reality of addiction. Others, however, do listen. Some judge us, some blame us, and some think we are out of our minds. We found that our main task is to act as conduits of God's grace. We leave the results up to God.

Our family would dare not dictate how other families must react. Each family situation is unique. For us, sharing has been therapeutic. For us, sharing has deepened our faith in God's ability to work in the lives of hurting people. God has awakened us to the reality that the people we encounter each day may be carrying heavy burdens. In living with addiction, families always walk the fragile, thin line between life and death. Our experiences have taught us that life is more precious and people are more valuable than we imagined. We see people in different ways than we once did. The homeless man under the bridge could have been our loved one had he not accepted recovery. We perceive the homeless with a different set of eyes, with a more compassionate heart than previously. Largely ignored by society, the mentally ill, who often suffer with addiction, have gained our respect and a soft spot in our hearts. We never take for granted that those sitting next to us in the pew are living easy lives. One never knows the difficulties with which our church friends live each day.

Addiction changed our lens of perception. Addiction created within us a sensitivity for those who are suffering, whatever the source or situation. Addiction instilled in us the gift of compassion.

As each family weighs the pros and cons of sharing their addiction stories, God also grants insight into how much to share. Time spent in prayer and discernment are tools God uses to guide us to our decisions. We may discover that not enough time has passed to prepare us for the readiness to share. The more time spent in addiction, the more our picture of addiction is altered. Our ability to share may be dependent upon time: time to process, time to heal, time to gain confidence in ourselves, and time to trust God to lead us. Hopefully, by examining some of the pros and cons of sharing, each family's decision can be ongoing as we work through the processes of addiction. Our primary discussion focuses on the benefits and hazards of confiding in fellow church members.

First and foremost, fear rules our reluctance to share with fellow church members. We fear that our integrity will be questioned and our respect diminished. Questions, derived from our fears, spill forth. How will church members react? What will they think of our family? Will they blame us? Will we be found guilty and condemned? Families in addiction live in a survival mode. We worry that if we tell our story, our acceptance and approval by church members will be destroyed. Because of our visibility as active leaders within our congregation, our fear and anxiety rises to a new level. Everyone knows our family; therefore, some people are bound to gossip and talk behind our backs.

Families of addicts take a risk anytime they share their story; this is a reality they must confront and learn to live with. They hope their church friends' reactions will be loving and supportive (or at least kind). Unfortunately, this simply does not always happen. Many of these church friends have no clue what they are talking about and the experiences we are facing. Others are ready to judge, blame, and condemn these family members the moment they open their mouths to speak. People once held to strict confidence may violate their trust. A few church friends—those very people they thought were trustworthy—may shock them with their vicious attacks. When faced with these unpleasant experiences, people with addicts in their families can leave worship some Sundays with shame on our faces, rather than gladness in our hearts.

Knowing that some church members would treat any family in such an unforgiving manner may upset our preconceived notions of "church." We are called to be the body of Christ. We are taught to love one another.

Our churches are comprised of fallible, sinful human beings whose misinformation and ignorance cause us to be the victims of their own self-righteousness. Be assured that some of our church members view addiction as a sin rather than a disease. They live with the false notion that addiction has a cure. They believe that if our addict *really wanted to quit*, he or she could. Most church members have little knowledge of addiction issues. Some think our families needed to exert better control over our addicts. Like Job's friends, church members may still hold to the outdated theological concept that God is punishing our family for past sins. To be fair to many of our fellow worshippers, they are simply not educated about addiction. Until addiction happens in their family, they never venture onto that playing field.

Presenting the negative side of sharing with church members proves just how fragile our sharing can become. The beast of malice quickly devours us, so we must tread carefully. Do not rush into our congregations to share and come away blind-sided because others do not understand or perhaps condemn or judge unfairly. We must be fully aware of the negative results of our sharing.

Strength for sharing, even in the midst of difficulty, comes when we place our family in the hands of God. As children of God, we embrace God's forgiveness even when our own church members do not offer their forgiveness. We speak out, with the assurance that our family bond is strong enough to withstand the winds of criticism. We have enough confidence in ourselves. We persist in our ability to fight off the arrows that attack us and weaken us. Our own self-respect carries us forward in our undaunted efforts to educate fellow church members about addiction. We are unstoppable, for our message has an urgent note. We never know which of our church families are walking the tightrope of addiction or which families may one day find themselves hanging from the high wire of addiction. So while we must weigh in with the negative, we must also believe that the risks of sharing can be countered when we accept our own self-worth as children of God.

Despite the unpleasant outcomes to sharing, families may come to the conclusion that they will be honest with church members. Before plunging head-on into sharing, family members must talk with their addict about the question of anonymity. Many recovery programs stress anonymity for the addict, just as the addict pledges to respect the anonymity of other fellow addicts. Stories told in recovery meetings remain there unless the addict chooses to share beyond the walls of the recovery rooms. Before we go blurting out our stories to others, we must hold a frank discussion with our addict. Get his or her opinion on how much to reveal. Have a blunt talk about the addict's comfort levels in terms of family sharing.

Some of us may be thinking that we do not owe our addict this respect. After what he or she has put us through, we may consider his or her opinion to be invalid. That said, if our addict has committed to recovery, he or she should be granted the privilege of anonymity. Be patient; a future time may come where our addict's confidence and self-esteem has been boosted enough in his or her program of recovery that permission will be given to share our experiences with anyone we encounter. Many addicts' lives are filled with unrelenting guilt and shame; give him or her some time to accept the gift of recovery and discover his or her own self-worth. Most addicts will probably allow us to share with some of our close church members. More freedom may be given to share when our addicts no longer live in our communities or when our addicts are working a recovery programs some distance from our homes. Removed from the situation geographically, our addicts do not come under as much pressure or strain of seeing these people on a regular basis, and therefore may grant us greater freedom to share. Keep in mind that strained relationships with our addicts may become inevitable if we break the promise of anonymity.

We walk a fine line between disclosure and silence. Anonymity plays a role in our ability to share. However, there are ways we can offer help to church members without disclosing the name of our addicts. If someone confides in us that they are seeking help for addiction issues, we can reveal to them that we also have a family history of addiction—without going into great detail. We must realize that given our knowledge of addiction issues and our ability to point individuals to competent resources, we provide people with clues that we have some background in addiction. Our addicts should not hold it against us that we helped another individual. As someone actively involved in programs of recovery, most addicts will begin to mature in their willingness to share and to have us share as well.

Given the viciousness of addiction, the time may come when our addicts blatantly refuse help and succumb totally to the forces of addiction. As devastating as this decision may be for our family, never forget that family members deserve the gift of recovery—with or without our addicts. We owe it to ourselves to get help even if our addict opposes help. We will learn, over time, that our own recovery entails the willingness to help others who endure the same plight. Helping others frees us from the selfishness addiction imposes on family life. At this point, we are left with the difficult decision of whether to go ahead and share with others so that we can open the doors of recovery for ourselves. After prayer and discernment, we give ourselves the permission we need to let go and share with church members, especially those we sense may be struggling with their own issues of addiction. We critically damage our recovery process when we do not accept the freedom to share and help others.

Clearly there is a fine line to be drawn. The addict refuses help, but we wish to reach out to others. We must tread carefully. The addict's right to privacy and anonymity outweighs our decision to share. Keep open the lines of communication with your addicted family member and do not share if he or she is adamant that you keep quiet. Securing the trust of your addict is far more important than your desire to share. If your addict is vehemently opposed to your sharing, talk only with a trusted friend, pastor, or couselor.

I am certainly not suggesting that we give up hope on our addicts, turn our backs on them, or go about our own business with no regard for their opinions. What I am saying is that there may come a point where an addict's addiction takes such a strong hold on his or her life that it is impossible for them to engage in competent decision-making. We have the God-given right to embrace recovery. Our addict's opinions on our family's anonymity and his or her say-so in the matter may have to be relinquished for the benefit of our family's recovery.

The addict in my family deserves a great deal of credit for allowing us to be open and honest about his struggles with addiction. We initially shared with a few close friends and our pastor. Our addict was aware that we had shared with these people. He sought out a pastor he could confide in, a pastor who himself had a history of addiction but had been sober for many years. As our loved one accepted his program of recovery, he now shares his story with other addicts. He also knows that we sometimes reveal his story to others with whom the message needs to be shared. Our addict's recovery hinges on his willingness to share his message with others. Giving unselfishly and sharing unlimited time and effort to help other struggling addicts are essential to his sobriety. Our family's recovery program also turns on our ability to offer help to others.

Addiction desires us to become and remain selfish individuals. The truth of the matter stares us in the face. As we relinquish our self-centeredness, we are released from the stronghold of addiction. I express appreciation to my addict for acknowledging this truth, both individually and as a member of our family. I thank him for giving us the freedom to discreetly share our family addiction story. I am humbled by the trust he places in us. My family is guided in our sharing by his trust and our unconditional love for him. Therefore, the responsibility falls upon us to share with integrity, never violating or diminishing the trust he has placed in us.

What have been the positive results from sharing that may inspire and motivate our families? Addiction prides itself on the secrecy it creates in family life. Getting our secrets out into the open, especially sharing with our trusted church friends, can be liberating. We find a weight has been lifted off of our shoulders. Sharing lifts the stigma associated with addiction. We are given opportunities to explain to our church friends the nature of addiction. Our revelations are an education for many church members. Our efforts often lead to positive results. We can advocate for workshops dealing with addiction and enlist help to start support groups sponsored by our congregation. We can spearhead the drive to obtain permission from church leaders to allow the use of the church space for recovery groups to meet.

When we are honest with fellow church members, we grant them the privilege of praying for us and supporting us. Prayers for our addict and family members would have been impossible had we not been willing to share our story. People in our congregation grow in their own faith when they are given the privilege to pray for others. We should not be afraid to ask people in our church family to covenant to pray for our family, our addicts, and for us. In our next chapter, we will discuss prayer in detail, but we have the assurance that the prayers of others will provide us strength for the many dark days we will face.

Sharing our addiction stories gives witness to the substance of our faith. We can testify to a God who is more powerful than addiction, even when addiction manifests itself as pure evil. We can demonstrate that regardless of the chaos of addiction, we live each day in the strength of God's power and not our own. We can claim God's unconditional love for our addict and ourselves. We can teach others that suffering produces patience and endurance. We can embrace pain with grace. Even while entangled in hopeless situations, we can cling to the source of our hope in God. When we are blamed, shamed, or have guilt placed on us by those in our faith community, we can learn to "turn the other cheek" or (as Job did) proclaim loudly our innocence. Our addiction story becomes transformed into a faith story when we allow the spirit of God to breathe new life into our dry bones.

Speaking of dry bones, addiction, like a vulture, picked us clean of the meat of our salvation. We found ourselves in the valley of dry bones in our relationship with God. Along the way, we fell into the deep crevices of spiritual neglect with no escape in sight. Our experience of worship was altered from glad worshipper to sad saint. I cannot speak for every family, but I can share with others the experiences of my husband. My husband felt as if he had entered a black hole from which there was no escape. When he entered God's sanctuary for worship, he came into it numb. He was worn out physically, emotionally, and spiritually. He was so tired that he stumbled through the motions of worship. Worship left him hollow and void. He lip-synched the hymns, he mumbled the liturgy, his mind wandered during the prayers, and he searched frantically for some word in the sermon that could lift him out of the mire of his depression. While the Scriptures spoke to him intellectually, they failed to speak to his hurting heart and his restless soul. With his energy level completely depleted, he found it challenging to interact with others worshippers and escaped into solitude as soon as the service was over.

Fellow church members who know my husband would tell others in no uncertain terms that I am exaggerating the truth. They are acquainted with an intellectual man, a man of deep faith, a solid theological thinker, and a man whose excellent Sunday school lessons have marked him as a distinguished teacher.

Through no fault of his own, addiction drove my husband into the valley of dry bones, just as it has driven many other people of strong faith. Others may not relate entirely to my husband's story, but each of us facing addiction can identify similar pieces of truth within our spiritual struggles. My husband courageously admits that it might take years before he can completely emerge from the valley of dry bones. Yet, he remains confident of the promise of God to transform the dry bones of his spiritual life. He abides patiently and calmly in God's time and in God's care. He continues to worship, praise, and serve God faithfully, knowing that God alone has the capability to restore the joy of his salvation. He points no finger of blame toward God; instead, he holds a mighty grudge against addiction. His wake-up call to the ravaging effects of addiction on his spiritual well-being urged him to sound a warning signal of caution for other families.

Trusting in God's ability to restore the joy of our salvation and earnestly believing in the power of God to breathe new life into our dry bones are both affirmations of faith. We cannot sincerely proclaim the good news of God's restorative power until we have dealt with the issue of suffering. God does not bring about suffering as a mean of punishment; yet interestingly, the children of God continually suffer in the biblical writings. In the midst of suffering, God redeems his people, offering them God's sustaining presence. Reading the Gospels, there is nothing to suggest that Jesus deliberately sought suffering or encouraged others to seek it, for that matter. The gospel writers capture a portrait of Jesus doing all He can to alleviate suffering. Jesus heals the sick, welcomes the outcast, comforts those who mourn, and strikes out against the forces of oppression. Even in Jesus's darkest hour, when the shadow of the cross loomed largely in His future, Jesus prayed earnestly to be delivered from that ordeal.

We too have prayed earnestly to be delivered from the ordeal of addiction, yet we have been summoned to face it head-on. Our courage derives from how we deal with suffering, not how we seek to avoid it. We believe in God's goodness, a goodness that is so much deeper than our suffering. In the face of adversity, Jesus models for us the courage that helps us to grow strong. Jesus was so rooted in God's love, just as we must be firmly rooted. Just as Jesus bore up under the cruelty of His suffering, we can find the bravery to bear up under the suffering of addiction. God is greater than our suffering, God is in the midst of suffering and He is more powerful than our suffering. The lesson of suffering is not the question of *why;* it is *how.* How are we going to deal with our suffering in such a way that we leave an open door for God's redemptive powers to flow through us and within us?

So we go back to our friend Job. Job teaches us a valuable lesson, one that is hard to swallow, however. Our world co-exists with both a loving God and terrible suffering. Job's friends try to convince him that he deserves his misery, just as many of our acquaintances will try to convince us that we deserve ours. Job cried out—as we often do—that he will not settle for the mystery of such unjust treatment as has been afflicted upon him. Does this sound familiar? In the end, God agrees with Job. The reasoning of his friends was wrong after all. Then God proceeds to offer Job a different kind of gift. God does not answer Job with a neat, packaged philosophy of suffering; instead, God offers Job the manifestation of His divine presence. There are no explanations given to counter Job's and our ranting, yet a distinct, clear call is sounded for Job and for us to stand up and exhibit courage in the face of the whirlwind. God offers Job and us no litanies of reasons for suffering; rather, God comes to Job and us as a sustaining presence in the midst of our suffering. God provides the same for each of us.

Each day of our lives, even in the whirlwind of our suffering, we see evidence of God's divine compassion. Even in the presence of overwhelming suffering, we must never reject the signs of God's love and goodness. These signs point to His presence with us always, often manifested in surprising ways. God sends people our way. These include individuals we would have not expected to show us a picture of God's love. Yet, we find God's love reflected in the face of strangers, in the faces of our family members, and in the faces of our church family. God never promises our lives will be devoid of difficulties; He offers us the grace that guides us and the courage that saves us as we live out and face our difficulties.

When our family's faith competes with our family's addiction, our beliefs are tested; our sacred stories are challenged. Our faith is grounded in a remarkable story, a biblical saga of a good universe brought into existence by a loving Creator God. In the history of creation, in the story of God's salvation, in the process of God's redemption of all creation, we proclaim that grace works through even the most addictive situations. Like Job, our friends, even our friends in the faith, do not have the last word. Like Job, we are silenced by the awesome, empowering presence of God Almighty who always has the last word. Our God speaks words of healing.

Like Job, we wait for God's redemptive powers to forcefully surround us. In God's presence, our questions cease just as Job's questions ceased in God's presence. These questions are meaningless when we are embraced by God's grace. Like Ezekiel, we wait for the dry bones to come to life. We do not wait alone, however. We wait, enveloped in a love that will not let us go, a love that suffers with us, a love that transforms our shadows of the valley of death into the light of the valley of life. Begin now; God invites us to walk forth from the valley of the shadow of death into the valley of life that awaits us on the other side of addiction. Our adventures begin when we take the first steps of faith and, as faltering and insecure as they may be, they are enough to begin to shatter the gloomy darkness of addiction.

CHAPTER FOUR:

If I Just Pray Hard Enough

"Give ear, O Lord, to my prayer; listen to my cry of supplication. In the day of my trouble, I call on you, for you will answer me."

Psalms 86:6–7 (NRSV)

Throughout the psalms, David—the shepherd boy turned king—cried out to God with heart-wrenching prayers. David, who wrestled with the enemies of his soul and who constantly worried about the enemies that pursued his nation, knew that he undoubtedly needed divine intervention. Reading the prayers of David in the book of Psalms, we immediately sensed a kinship with King David (even though as far as we know, David did not face any problems with addiction in his family). We are drawn to David and his prayers because we too have faced an enemy that pursued us, an enemy far stronger than we ever imagined we would encounter. David worried about the welfare and peace of his nation. David's enemies sought to tear apart the security of the land he ruled. The enemy of addiction wreaked havoc on our souls, tearing our security apart with the fierce determination to rule and dominate our family life. We worried about the welfare and security of our family, including that of our addict.

Like David, we also sought divine intervention. Like David, we cried out to God with ceaseless prayers of petition and supplication. Like David, we invoked prayers for healing, for safety, for protection, for grace, for peace, and for sanity. We prayed for courage and enough strength to survive each new day. We prayed that God would shower upon us enough sheer determination to meet our everyday struggles with fortitude. Surely David would have understood the myriad prayers we are compelled to pray. David was caught in the mire of his own troubles, just as we are caught in the snare of our family addiction. We share a bond with King David, a bond of restless days, sleepless nights, chaotic upheaval, and difficult decision-making.

As people of faith, we shared other cords of commonality with this man, even though we are separated from him by time, place, and life situation. King David trusted and clung to a God he believed heard—and answered—his prayers. If we are to claim any hope in our stories of addiction, we too must trust and cling to God. We must earnestly believe that God hears—and answers—our prayers. This assurance grounds us in our fervent belief. We settle for no half-hearted committal. We embrace our prayers with our whole hearts and with our whole being. Nothing less than our strong confidence in the power of God to hear and answer prayer will forge our kinship with King David, for he truly believed in God's amazing grace in his time of need, as must we.

That's easier said than done, however. One moment we discovered ourselves able to voice clear, thought-provoking prayers that ring out loudly from our mouths. Other days, we barely mustered enough energy to mutter prayers from exhausted lips and parched throats. In our frailty, we uttered our words; in our frantic need to be heard, we rambled on and on about our problems; and in our guilt, we acted as judge and jury. Because we were drained of energy, our prayers reduced us to embarrassed beggars before our God. We pled, we questioned, we accused, and we bargained with God. In our prayer times, we used every cliché in the book, recited every prayer we had been taught since childhood, and tested every prayer formula we could conjure up. We rationalized that our lack of faith kept our prayers from being answered; we often do characterize our prayers as "unanswered" and justify our thinking by our own excuses. We make a litany of reasons for our seemingly unacknowledged prayers. We stand up for God, but our utterances sound lame and silly. We tell ourselves God has important and vast concerns on a global level; therefore, our addiction issues must take a back seat along with our prayers. In the next breath, we blame God for failing us—for not hearing, for not answering, and for not caring.

Let us begin by affirming the biblical writers' promise through Scripture that God does indeed hear our prayers. Throughout the Bible, men and women of faith prayed with the unswerving conviction that God heard their prayers. God is a steadfast presence in our time of prayer even when we sensed a distance from God as we prayed. When we pray, we long to know God in an intimate manner, and when this does not happen for us, we conclude that God did not hear our prayers. Just the opposite is true: God's ability to hear our prayers is not dependent on how we feel. God's grace works to draw us back to Him. Our closeness to God in our prayer life is dependent upon our opening ourselves up to the Holy Spirit, letting God's Spirit infuse us with grace.

We place ourselves in an unhealthy position when we heap guilt upon ourselves. This guilt comes when we sense some distance from God in our prayer life. We must not allow addiction to convince us that God does not hear our prayers. Numerous times in the gospel records, Jesus demonstrates His unwavering faith that God hears our prayers. Otherwise, why would He spend time in prayer, often withdrawing to a quiet spot? This place could be your favorite room in the house, your place of worship, or a serene spot in nature. Why would He teach His disciples how to pray, thus providing us a beautiful model for prayer in the Lord's Prayer? The gospel writer Luke described the intensity of Jesus's prayer in the Garden of Gethsemane:

> *"In his anguish, he prayed more earnestly, and his sweat became like great drops of blood falling down on the ground."*
>
> *Luke 22:44 (NRSV)*

Jesus was at a crucial point in his life and ministry. Jesus faced impending arrest, trial, and crucifixion. He knew danger was on the horizon. Would it not have been ridiculous for Him to waste His precious time in prayer if Jesus thought God would simply turn His back on Him by ignoring His prayers? Jesus placed His full confidence in a God who heard His prayers. Jesus prayed, not mincing any words, but He approached God as Parent God, voicing His petitions openly, honestly, and with such fervor that His sweat turned into drops of blood!

Like the prayers of Jesus, our prayers flow from our trust in God and God's unfailing love. We must not think for one moment that God does not hear our prayers for our addicts and our family situations. We can offer our prayers with the full assurance that God remains by our side. God is not some remote deity who is not concerned for our family and us. We have God's full attention when we pray!

Probing further into the dimensions of prayer, we tackle this important question, a concern that has been gnawing away at us for some time: Does God actually answer prayers? Does God *hear* our prayers? Yes. We can give God credit in that regard. Does God *answer* our prayers? Now that is a totally different matter. In our desperate prayers, we plead with God to heal our addict of his or her dreadful disease. In our straightforward prayers, we agonize over why our addict refuses treatment. We beg God to lead our addict toward recovery. In our celebratory prayers, we thank God for any glimmer of hope. Then, in the same breath, we turn around and just to be on the safe side, utter a cautionary prayer, urging God to prevent relapse.

Unfortunately, for some of us, our prayer list has not advanced beyond praying for our addict to accept treatment. We dared not envy those families whose prayers have moved them forward to the realm of recovery. Yet, we wondered if our prayers have gone unanswered while other families of addicts have reaped the benefits of God's mercy.

For those of us who acknowledged answered prayers in the life of our addict, our prayers are pensive. We walk on tiptoes, waiting for the recovery bubble to burst. For this reason, our prayers often remain guarded. We never know how long we can make good on answered prayers.

My grandmother kept a plaque on the wall of her house throughout my childhood. It simply read, "Jesus answers prayers." As a child, those words offered me great comfort, as they still do today. In childlike faith, I run to God, trusting that God answers prayers. Yet, as an adult, my horizon has expanded to allow God to answer prayers—in His way and in His time. For several years, my husband and I prayed that our addict might be guided and directed to the right recovery center, that he would accept the help offered, and that he would begin a life of sobriety. At some centers, he failed to stay the course; he left before he completed treatment. Other times, he finished his ninety-day stay, only to relapse the moment he left. He would get in his car and drive immediately to the nearest liquor store. After his five bouts with pancreatitis, two grand mal seizures, and so many hospitalizations that the nurses began to recognize him, our family wondered if our prayers would ever be answered. Finally, through my husband's continuous and thorough research of recovery communities, we insisted that our loved one try again. Now he lives in a recovery community, works a diligent program of recovery, and against all odds, has turned his life around by embracing sobriety.

God answers prayers, but usually not in the way we expect. God's timeframe and ultimate purpose are beyond the realm of our comprehension. Learn to accept the mystery of prayer. What factors caused my loved one to decide to head in the direction of sobriety? There were so many colliding and weaving patterns that all my husband and I could do was stand back in amazement. There were the prayer warriors who devoted themselves to pray for my family members. Also, we had faithful friends who covenanted with us in lifting up my addict each day in prayer. Then, my loved one found a recovery community where fellow addicts demanded accountability and refused to give up on him. In addition, my addict turned his free will over to God.

God desires our addicts to become clean and whole. We serve a God who created us in God's image. God blessed all of creation and called it good. The Book of Revelation speaks of a new heaven and new earth, a time when all things will be renewed. Through biblical history, God is at work recreating fallen mankind. In the Garden of Eden, after Adam and Eve sin, God calls out to them and seeks to bring them back into a relationship with their Creator. We do ourselves a great injustice when we let others convince us that God has not answered our prayers because our addicts *deserve* punishment from God. We do not serve a God who delights in our suffering. We do not worship a God who forsakes our addict, abandoning him or her to suffering. God never wants any of us to wallow in the pit of addiction or suffer in anguish. God's purposes for the children created in God's image is that we would be whole, healed persons. Yet, let us not forget that God created us with the gift of free will. God cannot begin to answer our prayers and begin the process of healing our addict until our loved one is willing to surrender his or her will to God. Our addict's consequences result from poor choices and costly decisions to continue the addictive lifestyle.

Addicts cannot control their habits, but they can agree to get help. Our addict's moment of revelation came when he was lying on his carpet in his apartment in the middle of a seizure. He thanked God that at least he was on carpet and not on a hardwood floor! He awoke to the realization that he did not wish to continue life in this manner. We may never know why he grabbed sobriety at that time. It remains a mystery both to us and to our addict.

49

My family was humbled and awed by the mysterious nature of addiction. We continued to pray, in spite of the failures of our addict at recovery. Many avenues of recovery were made available to him, but he was not able to attain sobriety. He stayed at some of the best recovery centers; he worked with professional counselors, psychologists, and psychiatrists; and he attended competent support groups. Why he chose the path of sobriety one particular night on the floor of his carpet alone, in the midst of a seizure, goes far beyond our comprehension—and his. Were the prayers said on his behalf invalid or unheard? I do not believe so for one moment. Each of these prayers, each of the concerns and all the professionals, recovery centers, and support groups worked together, along with God's grace, to bring my loved one to the point of acceptance of sobriety.

God answers prayers. I cannot tell others why some addicts are healed through a religious experience, never to pick up the drug of their choice again. These miraculous healings fall far beyond the grasp of human thinking or reasoning, but I will testify that they are few and far between. Making this realistic observation should not diminish the miracle of a sudden, miraculous healing that defies logic. Yet, most families will spend a great deal of time in prayer before they see any visible results. This does not mean that God is not at work answering our prayers. Our prayers come to fruition in unexpected ways, places, and times. We practice faithfulness in prayer, waiting on God's time and not our own.

One way in which God answers prayers comes through the influence of others led by God to our addict. When my addict complained about all the money and time spent in recovery centers, I reminded him that these centers kept him alive. When he chastised professionals whom he claimed wasted his time, or when he judged his past sponsors as incompetent, I suggested to him that each person and each event had some role in his road to recovery. God brought these individuals and experiences into his life for a purpose. God answered prayers by guiding my family to the right places and introducing us to the people who influence our lives.

The Holy Spirit works behind the scenes of our lives to convict and lead. No doubt the Holy Spirit worked in the heart of my addict in ways I will never be able to comprehend or explain. I firmly believe the Holy Spirit was working in my husband's life as he diligently researched information on addiction, passing this along to our addict. The Holy Spirit gave people the right words to say (albeit words that my loved one sometimes ignored, words that often made him angry, and words that at times cut him to the core with their honesty). These words of advice were like seeds planted in his life. They took root and now are beginning to produce good fruit.

Looking back, I now know—without a doubt—that God sent angels to watch over my loved one. There were wrecked cars, but he escaped injury; close encounters with the law, but he was shown mercy; and such drastic abuse of his body that restored health seemed impossible, but eventually it did return. When one of his grand mal seizures put him in a coma, doctors told us if he lived (and that would not be likely), his body would remain in a vegetative state. Miraculously, he woke up the next day, surrounded by a host of gawking doctors.

Those individuals reading these words may be saying, "Hooray for the Hays family, but sorry, that is not my story at all," or "My daughter now sits in the county jail awaiting trial for heroin possession," or "My husband's alcoholism caused him to become so violent I had no choice but to throw him out of the house," or "My son now lives under a bridge somewhere." Did God grant us special treatment because were better Christians or more righteous prayer warriors than others? I am ashamed to admit that sometimes our faith was so weak and our prayers so shallow that the angel Gabriel could not have cracked our thick shells of doubt.

My family was the recipients of God's grace far beyond what we deserved. I wish I could offer a reasonable explanation as to why our loved one received an abundance of second chances. We were not more deserving than other families. I relate our experience to share the abundance of God's grace, the indwelling presence of God's Holy Spirit, and the mysterious yet miraculous timing of God's healing mercies. As people of faith, we are called to be people of hope. People who had worked with my addict told us that he was beyond hope, but in God's eyes, none of us is beyond redemption.

In no way do I want to leave my readers with false hope. Families of addicts live on a thin thread of hope, and we lap up any ray of hope offered us. Other families' outcomes may be totally different from mine. Their stories may end tragically, even with the death of a loved one. My own story is not completed; I have no way of knowing the final outcome. We hear so many sad stories and live through so many unhappy stories of addiction that I thought the people reading this book deserved a story of inspiration and an example of answered prayer. We had been praying for my loved one for many years, and we continue to pray for him. I have no way of knowing how God will answer the prayers in each family situation. Much depends on the attitude and actions of each addict and family member as he or she opens up to God.

Remaining faithful in our prayer life allows God's overshadowing grace, God's abiding presence, and God's comforting Spirit to permeate the dark places of our lives in remarkable ways we do not expect or anticipate. Daily prayer awakens us to the enveloping arms of God's mercy surrounding us at all times and in all situations. Sincere prayer releases our addicts into the hands of God and into the arms of others, those people who partner with God to help our addicts. Our patient prayers give God opportunity to work on His time schedule, not ours. If we could purchase a bottled prayer formula that would work in addiction, we would buy it at all costs, would we not? But no such magic "prayer formula" exists. Prayer, however, opens us up to the mysterious work of God in our lives, turns us into available and willing vessels to receive God's grace, and prepares and strengthens us for whatever lies ahead in our addiction journeys.

For this reason, I personally find great strength in sharing prayer requests for our addict with close friends, trusted church members, and our pastoral church staff. The letter of James instructs us to *"pray for one another, so that you may be healed. The prayer of the righteous is powerful and effective" (James 4:16 NRSV)*. We need to allow our community of faith the privilege of praying for us and with us. Asking for prayer requests for our family does not mean we have to share our entire stories or reveal all of our family secrets. As people pray for us, God knows our stories. God knows our secrets, even if the people praying for us lack the total picture. The Holy Spirit will anoint our prayer partners so their prayers on our behalf become effective. The Holy Spirit directs the prayers of those interceding for us. What a beautiful image we have of our families encircled by the prayers of God's people. Our families dwell in the arms of grace when access is granted for others to pray, interceding to God on our behalf. Inner strength and God's abiding peace will envelop our families when others offer prayers for us before the throne of God.

Unfortunately, our prayers for the healing of our addict do not always result in him or her being healed miraculously. Healing for addiction take many forms and shapes. We know there is no cure for addiction, but steps toward healing come when our addict commits to a lifetime journey of sobriety. Our addicts may totally reject recovery, but our families must not. Prayers are answered when we come alive to the realization that we must seek healing and recovery for our family even if our addict never arrives at this point in his or her life.

An awakening moment emerges when we obtain a mature definition of prayer based on the biblical tradition. Changing our attitude about the former way we defined prayer may guide us to a clearer vision of the role of prayer in the path of addiction. In times of poignant honesty, we admit that prayer has disappointed us. We fervently prayed for our addict, but some of us may have few results to show for our efforts; our addict still remains locked in the chains of addiction. Others rejoice in our addict's steady progress toward recovery, but we recognize our addict lives perpetually on the dangerous edge of relapse. We walk a day-to-day tightrope in our prayer life. Now is the time for an attitude adjustment in our thinking about prayer.

The biggest shift in our attitude about prayer develops when we trust God to be a vessel of resource for us. In contrast, we have expected God to throw us out a lifesaving raft of rescue in answer to our unremitting pleas. As we grow and mature in our faith, we move away from the concept of God as a *rescuer* and accept God as a *resource*. We free God to become our channel of available grace.

The shift in our thinking about God as a resource and steadfast presence in our addiction saga does not negate our prayers for rescue. However, our angle of vision and our attitude adjust when God is our resource. Our prayer requests call upon God to grant us grace and strength when we suffer. Our prayers ask God to help us live each day with patience and perseverance. Our prayers ask God to help us live in peace in the chaos of addiction. Our prayers center on our finding the tools and resources to endure whatever each day brings. Our prayers convey our obedience to God and a seeking after God's will. Our prayers reflect hope above despair and trust above fear. Our prayers speak of the unshakable faith we have in God. Our prayers tell us that we suffer in the presence of God, not alone. Our prayers allow us to discover that we are never disconnected from God and never without God's resources. Our prayers become a channel for God's Spirit to enter, working through us and within us. The Holy Spirit's indwelling presence surrounds us as we pray, inspiring us and strengthening us to deal with the challenges of addiction redemptively. In prayer, we manifest God's grace and open ourselves up to the resources of our faith.

There are some specific prayer requests that link families of addicts regardless of our specific situations. Let me share some prayer petitions that all families of addiction can express to God in our prayer times:

1. **Pray for the addict**

   Our prayer time is not the place to heap guilt and blame upon our addicts. Our prayer time is not the chance to accuse and belittle our addicts before God. Rather, we should pray that God will heal our addicts physically, spiritually, emotionally, and mentally. Addiction takes a toll on the entire body. When we pray this prayer, understand that, in most cases, healing (not curing) from addiction involves a long journey with many twists and turns. Inevitably there will be setbacks along the way. Do not think our prayers are unanswered if our addicts relapse. Do not try to force God into our impatient timing. As families of addicts, we want healing for our loved one immediately, the moment our prayers are finished; wait patiently in God's time. Many times, our prayers evolve into panicky pleas for help. If at all possible, enter prayer time calmly. Chaotic circumstances may prevent us from praying in a calm spirit. However we enter prayer time, we ask God to remove the panic and lead us to the serene waters of peace.

2. **Pray for recovery**

   Addicts need help to recover. Pray for our addict's willingness to seek help. Pray that our loved ones truly accept and embrace the gift of sobriety. Pray for our addict's efforts at recovery; getting and staying sober entails hard work. Pray that our addicts find recovery groups where they can work a strong program of recovery. When our addict becomes involved in just the right recovery community for him or her, pray for the members of that community, particularly our addict's sponsor. Having dealt with our addict, we all agree that his or her sponsor will most definitely need volumes of prayers! Affirm and compliment the addict for any progress. Offer prayers of thanksgiving to God. The majority of addicts relapse, so be prepared for this. When it happens, offer prayers that the loved one will start again on the road to recovery.

3. **Pray for family members**

   Each of our family members needs prayer during the trying times of addiction. Strong relationships with family can easily be severed when addiction enters the picture. Families are thrust into a whirlwind of change. Life centers on our addicts. Other family members take a back seat in our attention. Be aware that resentment will build when others are neglected and constantly starved for our attention. Pray to heal the broken relationships and painful rifts in our family life. Ask God to bring reconciliation and peace when there seems to be little hope. Pray for the guilt family members place upon themselves and the responsibilities they shoulder for the family addiction. Ask God to send the Holy Spirit to minister to these people and bring them the assurance that they are not guilty. Pray for family members who are shamed and disgraced by family addiction. Pray to be freed from enabling our addicts. Ask God to remove the addiction scars. Pray for children who live in addictive homes. Ask God to help family members seek recovery for themselves regardless of whatever choices the addict ends up making. Pray for family members daily by name. Tell family members that prayers are being said on their behalf.

4. **Pray for yourself**

Addiction saps us of our vitality and depletes our energy. Addiction strips us of the simple pleasures of life. Addiction is such a selfish disease that we clock in each day and clock out each night, based on our addict's needs, wants, and demands. Rarely do we take any time for ourselves. We never relax, so our bodies are tense and worn out. We live in a perpetual state of the chaotic. Addiction affects our bodies, minds, and spirits. We have, no doubt, noticed the poisonous venom of addiction's bite upon us. Depression, irritability, fatigue, and stress plague us daily. We should never feel guilty about praying for ourselves. Family members, especially those who shelter the greatest burden of addiction, become addiction caretakers. Ask God to give us the strength to take life one day at a time and the courage to face each day's challenges with grace. We are aided in this process when we give ourselves some credit. Most people would break under the heavy load we are carrying. Pray for God's guidance. Pray for wisdom, discernment, and fortitude. Pray for God to send people into our lives who will offer support and understanding, rather than criticism and ridicule.

5. **Pray for the needs of the world**

Addiction focuses our prayer life on our addict and our family concerns. Rarely do we pray about anything else. We rob ourselves of the joy of prayer when we become so self-centered in our prayer life. I would suggest that one begin prayer time by offering prayers of thanksgiving and praise. Thank God for the beauty of creation and the gifts of life. Thank God for His abundant blessings. Offer prayers for others in our social and faith communities who are struggling. Pray for healing for the myriad problems in our world today. Addiction cuts into the effectiveness of our prayer life when we think only of our family situation, forgetting the needs of others. Prayers lifted up for our community and world erases our tendency to be selfish in our prayer life.

Many beautiful and moving prayers have been written, but three stand out as being especially meaning for families of addicts. When we gather as a family, we will be unified as we read together these prayers from time to time. It also helps to commit them to memory so we can draw upon them when needed. I suggest these particular prayers because addicts in many recovery communities pray them. When we pray these prayers, we link ourselves with our addicts who will also voice these prayers in their own recovery programs. The three prayers are the Lord's Prayer (Matthew 6:9–13), the Serenity Prayer (credited to Reinhold Neibuhr), and the Prayer of Saint Francis of Assisi.

> *"Pray then, in this way: Our Father in heaven, hallowed be thy name. Your kingdom come, Your will be done, on earth as it is in heaven. Give us this day our daily bread, And forgive us our debts, as we also have forgiven our debtors. And do not bring us to the time of trials, but rescue us from the evil one."*
>
> *Matthew 6:9–13(NRSV)*

Those of us who worship regularly in a community of faith will probably already know the Lord's Prayer. Many of us learned this prayer as a child. The Lord's Prayer ties us to our faith community and God's people in every time and place. Many of the people who are praying for our families are individuals who recite the Lord's Prayer with us in worship. Saying this prayer in the Body of Christ reminds us that we need one another. We walk the journey of life with others disciples. Saying this prayer together in our family time reiterates to family members that they do not walk the addiction journey alone. Other families of addicts, who are also disciples, pray this prayer. Friends in the faith community pray this prayer.

So much of our prayer time consists in asking for what *we* want. The Lord's Prayer keys us into what God wants for us. We pray for the breaking forth of God's kingdom in full power and the accomplishment of God's Will here on earth. We pray for our basic needs, identified in the prayer as "daily bread." Then comes the part that speaks loudly to families of addicts. Jesus's prayer instructs us to forgive our trespasses as we in turn forgive the trespasses others have committed against us. Addicts owe our family a great deal in restitute, and we pride ourselves on reminding them of this from time to time. The Lord's Prayer calls us to forgive and to erase the debts of our addicts. Before we protest the injustice of this request, it is important to remember that forgiving our addict's many debts relates proportionally to whether our own debts can be forgiven. When we forgive, we open ourselves up God's reconciliation in our lives. In forgiving our addict, we are not saying that the injustices we have suffered are inconsequential to God. Rather, God is refusing to let addiction have the last word in our lives. We are invited to alleviate the vengeance that has smothered our joy. We release to God the crippling hold addiction has in our family life. The paralyzing chains of the unwillingness to forgive must be broken once and for all.

Forgiveness makes little sense to us; it is not natural to forgive. In forgiveness, we get back control of our lives. That is why Jesus commands us to replace retribution with forgiveness. Forgiveness is a gift from God. When we accept this gift by forgiving our addict, we send a loud and clear message that evil no longer has the upper hand. Evil no longer rules and controls our lives. In forgiveness, we are converted from angry, seething victims of addiction to forgiven and forgiving children of grace.

The Serenity Prayer is also a prayer of surrender, a prayer in which we give control of our lives and our will over to God.

> *"God grant me the serenity to accept the things I*
> *cannot change; courage to change the things I can;*
> *and the wisdom to know the difference."*

This prayer takes little time to learn. By memorizing it, I have found it comforting to say in times of stress. I have repeated this prayer not only during the troubled times of addiction, but also during the daily problems of everyday living. Of all the prayers we could say as families with addicts, I believe this one speaks prophetically to the issue of addiction.

We cannot change the fact that we have an addict in our family. Our addicts must commit to a rigorous program of daily recovery. We cannot erase many of the results of addictive behavior. For example, addiction specialists tell us that there is no cure for addiction. Addicts can decide to stop using and accept a program of recovery, but the battle of addiction lasts a lifetime. We know that we cannot force our addict to receive treatment. We certainly cannot work our addict's program of recovery for him or her, even though many of us have been determined to do so. As humbling as it is to admit, we did not cause our addict's addiction, we assuredly cannot control it, and we certainly cannot cure it. We cannot fix our addict although we have tried and our efforts resulted in failure.

In this prayer, we ask for the calming, peaceful gift of serenity that only God can give. We communicate to God that, in the past, we tried to control our addict's behavior. Like a skilled craftsman, we used the tools of enabling. Addiction manipulated our way of thinking. We thought our unconditional love for our addict could cure and control the disease of addiction. We were shocked beyond belief when we faced the truth that even our love could not conquer the unloving, relentless, all-consuming disease of addiction. Now we are ready to embrace the gift of serenity. We wrap ourselves in the blanket of serenity when we let God take control of the situations in addiction that previously defeated us.

At the same time, we are thankful beyond measure that some things can be changed in addiction. We turn to God for the courage to change our way of thinking and our way of acting. In prayer, God can change our attitude about our addict to the point where we are able to forgive. We will never forget the hurtful ways in which we have been treated, but we cannot let these injustices prevent us from forgiving. When we harbor resentments, they only build up inside us until we reach our boiling point. When we lay down our painful past to God, we pick up courage along the way. Courage is the tool we need to begin to change what can be changed and leave the rest to God.

With courage, we stop enabling our addict and start setting forth consequences, even sticking to them! Courage puts the daring words in our mouth, words that convey to our addicts that we will not support them any longer unless they agree to get help. Courage takes the past threats we were unable to enforce and turns them into swift action. With courage, we make the drastic decision to move our addict out of our home for our safety and protection. Courage provides us with the strength to put our loved one on a plane to a treatment center hundreds of miles away. Courage allows us put him or her in the helping hands of strangers. The families of addicts are some of the most courageous people in the world! Take courage and use this courage for all it is worth. Trust me, we will need it every single day as we deal with addiction in our families.

True wisdom comes to us when we are able to discern the difference between what we *can* and *cannot* change. Addiction muddies our thinking so that the lines of discernment are blurred together. Delineating between "changing" and "leaving alone" is difficult for families of addicts because our boundaries are skewed by addiction. Our sights are blinded and our vision is dimmed. In the Serenity Prayer, we petition God to clear our sight and to enhance our vision. Our addict has deceived us so much that we often cannot distinguish the truth from fiction. We pray for God's light to shine upon us, illuminating our way, giving us the wisdom to execute necessary changes—or the knowledge to refrain from unwise action.

The prayer of Saint Francis of Assisi contains biblical truths about giving, sharing, and receiving God's blessings.

> *"Lord, make me an instrument of your peace,*
> *Where there is hatred, let me sow love;*
> *where there is injury, pardon;*
> *where there is doubt, faith;*
> *where there is despair, hope;*
> *where there is darkness, light;*
> *where there is sadness, joy;*
> *O Divine Master, grant that I may not so much*
> *seek to be consoled as to console;*
> *to be understood as to understand;*
> *to be loved as to love.*
> *For it is in giving that we receive;*
> *it is in pardoning that we are pardoned;*
> *and it is in dying that we are born to eternal life."*

I have mentioned already that a dominant symptom of addiction is selfishness. Addiction pushes us to concentrate on the addict and his or her needs. Consumed by our addict's problems, we sometimes turn away from others outside our family, focusing all our time and energy on our addict and family crisis. This bold prayer challenges us to think outward, to do exactly the opposite of what we often find in the world around us.

We begin by applying this prayer to our relationship with our addict. Some of us are thinking that it would be a lot easier to start with outsiders. Most of these people— our friends, church members, co-workers, and even strangers—have not offended us nearly to the degree of our addict. They have treated us with more compassion and kindness than our addict has. Saint Francis's prayer of justice moves us to pardon our addict so we can receive God's blessings of joy, love, and peace. Through forgiveness, we pray that God will use us as instruments to bring reconciliation in difficult times. We should not pray this prayer if we are not serious about God taking our lives and using them to honor Him.

Recently, I was talking with our loved one as he shared with me his daily experience of prayer. He gets up every morning and falls on his knees for prayer time. He repeats this exercise each night before going to bed. Often he reads the Prayer of Saint Francis. He finds great meaning in the words of the prayer because he now understands the selfish nature of addiction. He knows that a huge part of his recovery process must be to get outside of himself and help others. Helping others aids in his recovery. When he sponsors a young person in his recovery group, shares at a meeting for addicts, goes out of his way to drive an addict to an event, or engages in a service project in the community, something powerful happens in his own life: he receives blessings.

Putting this prayer into action in our lives sets into motion an unfathomed boomerang effect. The principle makes no sense when addiction controls our lives. Hear the truth of what the prayer offers us as families of addicts: give, and we will receive blessings; forgive, and others will forgive us; love, and our lives will be filled with love. The vision of Saint Francis turns our worldly way of thinking upside down. Saint Francis's prayer brings to fruition exactly the opposite of what we find in our world; this prayer points us in the opposite direction from our experiences with addiction.

Addiction contains few seeds of hope and only distorted fragments of light. The result of addiction piles upon us despair, darkness, doubt, and hatred. Addiction fills us with overwhelming sadness, replacing our joy with fear. Addiction injures us so deeply that pardon seems unthinkable. As instruments of God, we reflect God's peace, love, pardon, hope, and faith in ways that turn our world upside down, especially our world of addiction. We cannot justify how this prayer works; we can only testify to the power of God to work in strange and mysterious ways in our world.

The Apostle Paul instructed the Christian community at Philippi:

> *"Do not worry about anything, but in everything by*
> *prayer and supplication with thanksgiving let your*
> *requests be made known to God, And the peace of*
> *God, which surpasses all understanding, Will guard*
> *your hearts and your minds in Christ Jesus."*
>
> *Philippians 4:6–7 (NRSV)*

These words of instruction from Paul initially sound ridiculous to families of addicts. Having dealt with nothing but worry and chaos, how could Paul have the audacity to tell our family to quit our worry and reside in peace? Peace and a worry-free life are diametrically opposed to addiction. Only a mature understanding of prayer makes possible what seems to us impossible. A faithful life of prayer for families of addicts rests in a God who will never forsake us and in a faith that draws from the well of God's grace. We pray, not in our own strength, for that strength fails us every time. We pray mustering all the strength that God provides. With confidence, we offer our prayers, knowing that the Holy Spirit is working, advocating for us, and blowing fresh winds of change into our prayer life. Above all, though, we pray in the powerful name of the One who endured suffering on a cross, the One who hours before this agony, prayed the most earnest prayer the world has ever heard.

Throughout his life, Jesus remained obedient to the Father, so it was only fitting that His last prayer be one of total obedient and submission:

> *"And going a little farther, he threw himself on the*
> *ground and prayed, 'My Father, if it is possible, let*
> *this cup pass from me; yet not what I want, but what*
> *you want.'"*
>
> *Matthew 26:39 (NRSV)*

Through no fault of God's and no fault of our own, the cup of addiction did not pass us by. Yet, the cry of Jesus must never pass us by unnoticed. Our prayers too must end with the same cry Jesus uttered: "Yet not what I want, but what you want." Never was it God's will for our loved ones to become addicts or for our families to be filled with addiction. Yet, by invoking these words of obedience and submission in our prayers, we release God's redemptive power to begin its work in our families and in the life of our addict.

By the way, I suspect our prayers, prayed in this manner, would bring a great deal of pleasure to our friend and ally, King David. I can just imagine King David rallying around our family, joining us in a prayer or two. Even if David cannot be present, do not worry. We are never alone in our prayer time. Christ's comforting presence surrounds us, God's ministering angels listen attentively, and the Holy Spirit carries our prayers directly to the throne of God. In the past, we may have dreaded our prayer times. They were like heavy weights upon us. We did not know what to pray for or what words to say. God's true desire for us in our prayer time is not that we concern ourselves with reciting pious words, but that we speak sincere words that flow from the depth of our hearts. We say our prayers believing that God hears our prayers and answers them in His correct time and purposeful manner. A mature faith accepts the mystery of prayer.

Pray, though. Pray hard and pray long. Pray like our very lives and the lives of our addicts depend on our prayers; they do! For without prayer, our families, our addicts, and we as individual believers disconnect ourselves from the lines of communication with Almighty God. So, come with the posture of humility and bow down before God, who longs to be in conversation with us. Come as trusting children of God and I guarantee us that our prayers will evoke smiles from heaven and nods of approval from the saints who witness our prayers with great joy.

CHAPTER FIVE:

If I Acted Better: The Children of Addicts

"Noah, a man of the soil, was the first to plant a vineyard. He drank some of the wine and became drunk, and he lay uncovered in his tent. And Ham, the father of Canaan, saw the nakedness of his father, and told his two brothers outside. Then Shem and Japheth took a garment, laid it on both their shoulders, and walked backwards and covered the nakedness of their father; their faces were turned away, and they did not see their father's nakedness. When Noah awoke from his wine and knew what his youngest son had done to him, he said, 'Cursed be Canaan; lowest of slaves shall he be to his brothers.'"

Genesis 9:20–25 (NRSV)

We are first introduced to Noah and his family in the biblical text when God instructed Noah to build a huge boat in preparation for a great flood that wiped out all the earth. Portrayed in earlier chapters of the Bible as a diligent ark-builder, compassionate rescuer of animals, and righteous friend of God, we are shocked in this passage to find Noah flat-out drunk on his face. God washed the world squeaky-clean, set the promise of the rainbow in the skies, and made a lasting covenant that included the animals along with mankind. Noah emerged from the ark, set his feet on dry ground, planted a vineyard, got intoxicated, and ended up in a drunken stupor.

Our immediate reaction is to make excuses for God-pleasing Noah, rationalizing that there is absolutely no evidence presented in the biblical text that Noah was an addict, which as far as we know is true. He simply had "one too many." Given what Noah had been through, we allow him the benefit of the doubt, telling ourselves he probably "deserved a few rounds."

We are drawn to the image of Noah lying drunk on his bed because his story reeked not just of homemade wine but of our own humanity as well. We neglect the problematic side of the story—where the younger son Ham received the brunt of his father's wrath when Noah awoke from his drunken sleep. Children raised in alcoholic homes might have an easier time recognizing this incident as one of the earliest stories of what happens when alcohol gets introduced into family life. Ham shared the struggles of any adolescent who has dealt with an intoxicated parent or a parent high on drugs. Ham must decide how to react to his father's drunken behavior. Should he cover his father's nakedness, ignore it, or run to his older siblings for help? Children of addicted parents know all too well the dilemma of whether to cover up or leave uncovered the secrets in the family. Ham followed in a long line of children forced to endure the wrath of a parent whose behavior embarrassed the rest of the family.[1]

Biblical interpreters justified Noah's actions, either blaming Ham for getting his older brothers to do the dirty work or belittling Ham for looking on his father's nakedness in an inappropriate manner. Even if there is an element of truth to these accusations, the end result is the same: Noah reacted with fury and outrage, leaving Ham to bear the scars of his father's curse for the rest of his life.

Children whose parents are addicts endure the curse inflicted upon them daily. They live topsy-turvy lives. In order to grow into healthy, mature adults, children need dependable parents and an environment of affirmation and security. Rarely does this happen in a home situation where one or more parents struggle from addiction. In these homes, children of addicts live behind the closed doors of their shame and guilt. Abandoned by one or more parents, these children confront too early in life adult issues that are thrust upon them, including issues of trust and self-worth. Forced to keep secrets, they carry into adulthood the emotional scars, leading to fractured relationships with others. Their very survival is often dependent upon their assuming the role of caregiver, which often forces them to abdicate their own childhoods in the process.

Children of addicts are robbed of the opportunity just to be children and revel in the pleasures of childhood that many children enjoy. They are forced to grow up quickly, pushing their own needs aside for the addict in the family. There is no time to be a child when survival dominates every waking hour and when hidden fear rules the night. Childhood takes a back seat to the power of addiction. The dark shadows of powerlessness snuff out the innocence of childhood when addiction enters the home.

What at first glance might appear to be only childhood issues of survival are very much faith issues as well. How can children be expected to trust in God when they cannot trust the very adults God has placed them with? Will God abandon them like their addicted parent does when he or she leaves these children alone to fend for themselves? If parents cannot be trusted, then perhaps God cannot be trusted as well.

A child grows in trust when the child's caregivers are trustworthy. A baby comes into the world completely dependent on others to meet his or her needs. As the baby's physical and emotional needs are met, so are his or her spiritual needs. When adults show love and compassion, God by association must be a loving and compassionate God. When caregivers are trustworthy, in the child's heart and mind, God is viewed as a trustworthy God. What happens to a child's image of a trusting God when over and over again, a child faces abandonment or cannot trust a parent to care for his or her needs?

Such questions can easily arise in homes where addiction dwells. In these homes, an addicted parent may not be physically or emotionally able to care for the needs of the child. The cries of a baby go unanswered by the addicted parent passed out on the couch. Sick with the disease of addiction, a parent can barely make it out of the bed to prepare the child's breakfast. Perhaps they lack the strength to help the child dress for school. A non-addicted parent feels compelled to give so much attention to the addict in the home that the child lacks Mom or Dad's attention.

What is it like for children in addicted households? In one home, a child routinely puts his alcoholic mother to bed, while in another, a child constantly checks her sleeping overdosed father to make sure he is still breathing. If we were given a view into the window of one home where an addict lives, we would catch a glimpse of a child cowering in his closet, not trusting the drug-induced state of his mother. In another window, we watch in horror the face of a child brave enough to shelter his mother against the physical blows of his alcoholic father. At a third house, though, we are left in the dark; all is hidden from our view. The blinds are shut fast and the curtains are completely drawn, concealing behind the walls of this house the family secrets of addiction.

Some of these homes contain children who leave their houses each week to attend church. After worship or Sunday school, they leave the safety of their churches, carrying in their hearts and minds the lessons taught them about a trustworthy God. On the way home, they sing catchy tunes about a loving God. They walk into their rooms quoting scripture about a protective Parent God. Yet these children return to homes where they cannot trust their own parents to offer them love and protection.

Some of us are children of addicts who have reached adulthood. We now struggle to reconcile the theology of a Parent God with our own experience. Others of us are the spouses of adult children of addicts. As young children and teenagers, our spouses—who were raised in addictive homes—bring into our marriages the devastating effects of addiction. We know firsthand the toll addiction has taken on our spouse's physical and emotional well-being. We understand the ways addiction has robbed our spouse of the joy of his or her faith. We remain secure in our own faith, but we long for the day when our spouse can remove all of his or her inhibitions toward God. We wait patiently for the time when our spouse will fully embrace the totality of God's love and grace in his or her life. Given our spouse's childhood history of family addiction, we understand, but regret, his or her reluctance to let go of the past. Unfortunately, some of us who are children of addicts are now married to addicts ourselves. The pattern of addiction we witnessed in childhood now plagues our married life.

Each of us must work together compassionately to help children of addicts develop the concept of God as a loving, trustworthy parent despite past or present experiences. Our starting point is a theology of a God we can absolutely trust and always depend upon despite our external circumstances. This God never abandons the children of addicts, but constantly abides with them in the messiness of life. Children of addicts bear both the physical and emotional marks of abandonment. Symptoms of physical abandonment include inadequate meals, lack of proper healthcare, safety issues, and in some cases, physical or sexual abuse. Emotional abandonment runs the gamut of parental indifference to children's needs and wants, unjustified parental blame, undeserved parental criticism, and lack of parental support and praise. We must reinforce to the children of addicts that God was never removed from them, even if their parents were absent. God is a Parent God who never abandons us. God is parenting us from the moment we are born and continues to parent us until the moment we die, and even into the realm beyond this present life.

Children of addicts fight a lifelong battle with trust issues. Given the lack of trust in their addictive homes, they find it difficult to trust anyone, including God. Proverbs 3:5–6 assures us that our God can be trusted with the direction of our lives, but we must reach out and respond in faith with our own affirmation of our trust in Him.

> *"Trust in the Lord with all your heart, and do not rely*
> *on your own insight. In all your ways acknowledge*
> *him, And he will make straight your paths."*
>
> *Proverbs 3:5–6 (NRSV)*

The writer of Proverbs directed us to trust God with our whole being. We are not to depend on our own understanding about our circumstances in life. Children of addicts know that in the case of addiction, there is no way to fully understand why others got the pleasure of living a carefree childhood while they endured a miserable one. Who can ever explain the injustices of children who have to assume adult responsibilities? As children of addicts begin to trust and acknowledge God in their lives, He begins to work in their lives to bring healing. Only God can make straight the path of a life that addiction has made crooked. Only God can guide the direction of a shattered life so the child of God can walk with dignified steps rather than with sluggish feet.

Children raised in addictive families often learn that it is unsafe to trust others. With God's help, these same children can trust Him and others who are friends in their community of faith. One of the family rules in addiction instructs children to keep quiet and not talk. Children learn to rein in their emotions. Some children of addicts will confess that they were taught not to think—and definitely not ask—about what was happening in family life. Addiction is an illness that destroys a person's ability to enter into relationships with others. Children of addicts have a difficult time establishing and sustaining meaningful relationships. When these children are a part of a community of faith, or even in their dating, marriage, and family relationships, they may encounter mental, physical, and emotional blocks that prevent them from opening up to others.

Friends in the community of faith must be especially sensitive in understanding that children of addicts need time to trust others in the same way they need time to trust God. We often speak of the "family of God" as descriptive of our congregations. The phrase "family of God" can either offend or attract the children of addicts. Some children of addicts want nothing to do with those who call themselves a *family*, because they are afraid the church might reflect their family life. On the other hand, some children of addicts may find great comfort and appeal in the idea of the church being a family of God because they have never experienced the warm, caring atmosphere that a church family can offer. We must be sensitive to the way we use the phrase "family of God," and the way we live out in the community of faith. The task of the church is to model "family of God" in such a way that children of addicts find our church family of God an environment of safety, love, and respect.

As brothers and sisters in Christ, we can surround the children of addicts with a loving, caring environment that is diametrically opposed to what they may have experienced or may be experiencing in their family life. We can surround them with a community of faith that accepts and loves them for who they are. We must not blame them or place guilt upon them for the family addiction. Trust me: they will do an excellent job of heaping blame and guilt upon themselves.

Helping children of addicts establish a predictable and reliable routine in church life counteracts the unpredictability they have known in their own families. Established routines such as sitting down to dinner or being put to bed with a bedtime story are often unrealistic hopes for children of addicts. They never know if the addict in their family will even show up for dinner. The addict may garner all of the attention so there is no time for a bedtime story or any regular bedtime ritual. If home is a place of uncertainty, chaos, and turmoil, in contrast, church must be a place of certainty, security, and peace.

The Christian calendar offers the children of addicts the predictability of the faith story, a story re-enacted each year in the life of the church as believers journey through the seasons of Advent, Christmas, Epiphany, Lent, Easter, and Pentecost. These holy seasons introduce children of addicts to a God who dwells with them in all the seasons of life in amazing and powerful ways. The church seasons provide a constant rhythm to life, in contrast to the inconsistency of life for children of addicts. Children of addicts eventually run into ordinary time, a time outside of the holy seasons. Here they encounter a God who meets them in the mundane tasks of everyday living. These ordinary days can very well be filled with danger for children of addicts. Ordinary days may consist of hurt and pain. The church teaches them that God is present with them in the ordinary days of life, even when they turn out to be anything but ordinary.

Children of addicts often dread the holidays and other special occasions because in their childhood, these were anything but pleasant. Most of us remember with fondness our family gatherings, especially during occasions such as Christmas and Easter. We enjoyed a delicious family meal, conversed and played with our relatives, listened to family stories passed down from generation to generation, and delighted in opening presents. Children of addicts may remember family dinners that were spoiled by a drunken or over-drugged parent, yelling and screaming among family members when the drunken relative fell into the Christmas tree, the failure of a parent to show up for a birthday party, and tears mixed with disappointment when family rituals were shattered.

These sorts of rituals usually break down in families destroyed by addiction, so it is difficult in adulthood for children of addicts to establish their own family rituals. In the same way, it may be challenging for children of addicts to embrace with great enthusiasm the rituals and special events of the church and faith. When we empathize with them and show kindness and compassion, children of addicts can be guided slowly through each event and ritual. We must help them to see that there is no need for disappointment, anxiety, or fear. Over time, with patience and love, the children of addicts can come to trust in the rituals and events of the faith as dependable.

In contrast to their own family rituals, the powerful rituals of the church in baptism and Holy Communion invite children of addicts to enter into a relationship with a God who reaches out to them in love and grace. As children of addicts witness or participate in these rituals in the community of faith, they are drawn into a relationship with a trusting, dependable God who will never abandon them. As they come face to face with holy and sacred moments within the life of the church, the negativity they experienced with rituals in their childhood may not disappear, but it will be replaced by positive experiences with new rituals that are trustworthy and dependable.

Children of addicts learn over time to expect to be disappointed, because events probably would not turn out positively. When parents fail to show up for their sporting events and their school activities, or when they receive no praise for their good grades, these children learn not to expect affirmation. Over time, some children can build up walls of defense, pretending they do not need praise. Some individuals act hard and cold toward others so that friends and spouses may find it impossible to permeate the shells of their toughness. Others seek out people who will offer them any measure of praise and affirmation, sometimes choosing people who do them more harm than good.

Being aware of this, we in their communities of faith should express to them praise and affirmation for jobs well done. We may have to offer it in small doses at first so as not to overwhelm them. We should not be surprised if our words of praise are met with blank stares or unbelieving glances. We may receive a lukewarm "thank you" or no response at all. Children of addicts, starved for attention and praise, but not having received any, will often turn inward. They know not how to react to our words of kindness. Be patient and keep affirming these children of addicts as people of worth.

Children of addicts have had their self-worth squashed so much that eventually they come to view themselves as worthless. Therefore, these children live with shame. Guilty feelings arise when the child faults him- or herself for an inability to bring any relief to the family situations. For example, the young child reasons that if he or she had acted better, perhaps his parents would not drink so much. An older sibling may take on the responsibility of protecting a younger sibling, but he is riddled with guilt when his younger sibling receives inadequate care. A child bottles up his or her guilt when he or she gives excuses to friends as to why playtime is impossible. The child knows he or she must get home to check on an addicted parent. The child comes to learn that inviting friends over to play can become too risky. When these children have no control over their lives or their family situation, their self-esteem is lessened. Shame and guilt work together effectively in their negative ability to destroy a child's self-worth.

Our faith teaches us that we are people created in God's image and that we are valuable to God. The Scriptures reveal to us a God who knows us by name and who has a wonderful plan and purpose for each of our lives. Children who live with addiction often have a hard time believing God knows their names, cares about their situation, or has a plan and purpose for their lives. The prophet Isaiah spoke to his people at a time in which the nation needed the assurance that God was with them. Isaiah depicts God as Creator, Redeemer, and One who knows their names.

> *"But now thus says the Lord, He who created you,*
> *O Jacob, He who formed you, O Israel: 'Do not fear,*
> *for I have redeemed you; I have called you by name,*
> *you are mine.'"*
>
> *Isaiah 43:1 (NRSV)*

The Isaiah passage assures the children of addicts, as it did the Children of Israel, that God is present in their times of exile. God is available to them in those situations where home is anything but a warm and cozy environment. As children of addicts become adults and strive to rebuild lives that have been destroyed by addiction, they can move forward in the redeeming care of a God who knows them by name.

I do not want to leave others with the impression that children of addicts cannot function in life; this is far from the truth. Some children of addicts have the ability to detach themselves from the addiction scene and find meaningful relationships outside of the home. These resilient children remove themselves from the more damaging effects of addiction. Churches can be places where meaningful relationships are established for these children. Sunday school teachers, pastors, and church friends can be relied upon to offer support not found in the home.

The non-addicted parents of a child being raised in a home where addiction is present carry additional burdens. They confront the dual tasks of dealing with addiction and parenting at the same time. I would urge these people to seek out the resources in their neighborhoods and their faith communities. They can turn to and rely on trusted friends who share their faith in God. The reality we face is that many people in our faith community will not understand much about addiction. We must accept this truth and not be too harsh on others for judging us unfairly or failing to comprehend our crisis. Turning to support groups in the community, where we can meet others who walk our same journey, offers us needed support which others may fail to provide.

The church friends of parents caught in the cycle of addiction can offer their prayers and support. Encourage this family (or any family like them) to become or remain active participants in the life of the congregation. Go out of your way to provide transportation for the children to attend church events when a parent cannot bring the children. Find ways to relieve the non-addicted parent so he or she can have a few hours of free time. Advocate for workshops to educate church members about addiction and support groups in our church and community to sustain families.

Reach out to the addict as well. The costs for quality treatment for addiction are very high. Churches might consider providing financial assistance for a family that cannot afford the expense. The apostle Paul reminds us of our obligation as brothers and sisters in Christ to take upon ourselves the pain and struggles of others and offer them some relief.

> *"Bear one another's burdens and in this way, you fulfill the law of Christ."*
>
> Galatians 6:2 (NRSV)

Experts who work with children of addicts define certain family roles that children gravitate toward and take upon themselves. Children may favor more than one role, depending on how many siblings are present in the household. While these family roles can be present in families where there is no addiction, they are prominent in addictive families. The underlying feelings that result from playing these roles are issues of faith. Many of these issues I have already addressed in this chapter, and I have tried to offer some biblical scriptures and sound theology to counteract these human emotions.

Children of addicts will quickly identify their family role from this list. As they study some of the traits, parents of addicts can begin to match their children's behavior in family life with certain roles that define children of addicts. Friends, church members, or pastors who know families facing addictions can use this summary, as it will provide information about the dynamics of addiction in family life, the role of children in the family, and the faith issues that emerge.

The Responsible Child

The responsible child, often the oldest sibling, becomes adept at bringing order and structure to the chaotic household of addiction. As these children assume adult responsibilities in the home, they are trying to make up for the inadequacies of the parent or parents. They have been known to clean the house, feed the other siblings, and take on other adult duties. There is little time for play. There is no way to function as a normal child. These children become "little adults" and allow themselves no time to relax. Their one goal becomes that of directing the household toward security, order, and structure. When these children enter adulthood, they continue to deal with control issues. They find it almost impossible to relax and enjoy life. They lack spontaneity and the ability to listen to others. They fear making mistakes, must always be right, and are inflexible toward the faults of others.[2]

Some of the faith issues with which these children struggle are those of fear, control, guilt, and shame. The responsible child needs to understand that God is in control of his or her life. They must learn to give up the control of their unmanageable household and their unmanageable life over to God, who is the only One who can take control and bring sanity into the insanity of family life. We all make mistakes. As a responsible child, this individual must learn to forgive others, exert patience toward them, and forgive his or her own misdeeds.

As perfectionists, these children continue to pile guilt and shame upon themselves when everything in their life does not go according to plan. No human being is perfect. The problem comes when we expect perfection either from ourselves or from others. When we try to control our lives and the lives of others with a perfectionist drive, we abdicate our role as human being created in God's image. We are humans; we are not God. Perfectionists unmistakably and often unknowingly try to play the role of God, an impossible task. The responsible child must learn to relax and enjoy each day as a gift from God. This happens when the child grants God control, quits harshly judging others, and accepts him- or herself as an imperfect, yet forgiven, child of God.

Here are some verses of Scripture for those people whose family role is characterized as responsible child:

> "*Light is sweet, and it is pleasant for the eyes to see the sun. Even those who live for many years should rejoice in them all ...*"
>
> *Ecclesiastes 11:7–8a (NRSV)*

> "*Do not worry about anything, but in everything by prayer and supplication with thanksgiving let your requests be made known to God.*"
>
> *Philippians 4:16 (NRSV)*

> "*Bear with one another and, if anyone has a complaint against another, forgive each other; just as the Lord has forgiven you, so you must also must forgive.*"
>
> *Colossians 3:13 (NRSV)*

> *"And be kind to one another, tenderhearted, forgiving one another, as God in Christ has forgiven you."*
>
> Ephesians 4:32 (NRSV)

> *"Finally, be strong in the Lord and in the strength of his power. Put on the whole armor of God, so that you may be able to stand against the wiles of the devil."*
>
> Ephesians 6:10–11 (NRSV)

The Adjuster

As the name implies, this child adjusts to whatever happens. This child reasons that he or she cannot do anything about the family situation, so there is no use in trying to prevent or alleviate the problems. We might find this child simply going to his room and shutting the door when arguments start. The adjuster is often the less-visible child who may spend time away from home with friends. If a child is told by his mother that he cannot attend a friend's party, rather than getting mad, crying, or arguing, this child will just accept the situation without much feeling or emotion. The opposite of the responsible child, the adjuster goes out of his way to avoid situations where he or she must take control.[3]

These children never have opportunities to develop trust or healthy relationships, the tools essential in developing a mature faith. Growth in our faith comes when we seek out healthy relationships with God and with others. A main characteristic of the adjuster child is that he or she fears making any decisions. Our faith requires us to make decisions. We make the decisions to put God first in our lives, to follow God's leadership, and to put our faith into action. Our faith instructs us to seek diligently the truth according to God's Word. We are not called to follow without questioning, which the adjuster child tends to do; we are to ask questions and seek answers. Our faith is a searching faith, not a faith that simply accepts whatever is told us without our probing and seeking for answers.

When conflicts occur in church settings, in home life, or in one's faith journey, the adjuster child handles the chaos by self-negating and ignoring it. He or she expresses no opinion and does not get involved in the crisis. This particular child finds "comfort" from living and existing in a constant state of agitation, which the adjuster child considers as a sign of normalcy. However, as an adult, the adjuster finds him- or herself dealing with depression, isolation, and loneliness.

Pastors and friends of the adjuster child may be frustrated when this individual cannot seem to make a decision. We must be especially patient and affirming of this child. Remember that in the Wesleyan tradition, God's grace reaches out to each of us. God's justifying grace helps us to commit ourselves to God. Trust this child to God's loving care. Place this child with mature Christians who can give solid biblical and theological answers.

The adjuster children must always be reminded that they are the beloved children of God. They cannot hide from God as they often hide from others. The Scriptures tell us that God knows all about us. He hears our innermost thoughts. When we cannot open up honestly with others, at least we can attempt to open up to Him in prayer. These children must strive to refrain from holding back their thoughts from God, but work to grow in their honesty with Him. They must believe that God knows their exact thoughts and welcomes them sharing these reflections with their God. They have to overcome the fear and anxiety of making decisions about their faith. When they find this difficult to do, I would advise them to seek out mature Christians who can help with any struggles. Do not rely on the advice of just anyone, however, especially those people with an immature faith. Do not be afraid to approach God; bring Him the questions of faith. Maturity comes as we probe into the depths of our hearts and ask the difficult questions. God will not judge these children or think any less of them as they search for answers. He will send the Holy Spirit to guide each one as he or she seeks direction and guidance in their lives.

When adjuster children face the times of loneliness and isolation, they are never alone. God is always present, especially in the fearful times of decision-making. Adjuster children are anchored in God's love and grace. Due to their home life of addiction, these children seek refuge and safety in the background. As cherished children of God, these children can now step forward and receive His love. God chooses each of them for a purpose, and they will never know their true destiny until the decision is made to follow in God's ways.

Here are some verses of scripture for the adjuster child:

> *"I am confident of this, that the one who began a good work among you will bring it to completion by the day of Jesus Christ."*
>
> *Philippians 1:6 (NRSV)*

"Because if you confess with your lips that Jesus is Lord and believe in your heart that God raised him from the dead, you will be saved."

Romans 10:9 (NRSV)

"'For surely I know the plans I have for you,' says the Lord, 'plans for your welfare and not for harm, to give you a future with hope.'"

Jeremiah 29:11 (NRSV)

"For God did not give us a spirit of cowardice, but rather a spirit of power and of love and of self-discipline."

2 Timothy 1:7 (NRSV)

"For you did not receive a spirit of slavery to fall back into fear, but you have received a spirit of adoption. When we cry, 'Abba! Father!' it is that very Spirit bearing witness with our spirit that we are children of God, and if children, the heirs, heirs of God and joint Heirs with Christ ..."

Romans 8:15–17a

The Placater

The placater describes that sensitive child in the family of addiction whose feelings are more easily hurt than those of others. This child copes with the problems of addiction by fixing. The child exerts a great deal of energy trying to resolve the tensions, fears, angers, and sadness of his siblings and parents. The placater child works hard to make life easier for others in the home. If Mother embarrasses his sibling in public due to her drunken behavior, the placater child will soothe the hurts and embarrassment of his sister. When his brother is angry with Dad for breaking his promise to attend his baseball game, the placater child dispels his brother's anger.

As the placater children reach adulthood, others perceive them as "nice" persons. We are drawn to them because of their caring nature, their good listening skills, and their warm sensitivity to others. The placater constantly apologizes for the slightest wrong and rarely disagrees with anyone. Busy taking care of everyone else's emotional needs, the placater loses the ability to receive care from others and fails to focus on his or her own needs. They shy away from anger and controversy. They are often lonely and depressed because they do not believe they deserve to have equal standing when it comes to relationships.

The pastors, church members, or friends of the placater child can help him or her grow in faith when thanks are extended to these children for loyal service rendered to the church. Yet, we also do these children a great favor when we insist that placater children find methods of relaxation. People who have contact with placater children should insist that they find time to allow others to take care of them. Watch them and be careful they do not overburden themselves with service to others. Place them in relationships with others with whom they have equal status.

The Scriptures commend many of the qualities possessed by the placater child. Our faith teaches us to strive to be sensitive to the needs of others, to listen carefully to the concerns of others, and to give ourselves unselfishly in service to others. Placater children are to be praised for the many virtues that the Bible lifts up as pleasing to God. Servant leadership, held in high regard by our biblical writers, characterized the life of Christ. However, God also wants each placater child to be willing to receive from others. These children have to be encouraged and taught to allow their family, friends, and church members to bless their lives. They must come to a full understanding that they rob others of the joy of giving to them when they fail to grant others the privilege of sharing with them.

The guilt these children carry stems from not being able to please others all the time. None of us is perfect. Striving to please others all of the time is an impossible task. These placater children will only become weary. Because they fail to accomplish all they set out to do, they can be plagued by guilt. Placater children can also be filled with guilt when people fail to respond as these children desire. No good is accomplished when placater children punish themselves with guilt feelings because others did not show them the appreciation or praise they felt justified to receive. God desires to take away their guilt and replace it with His abundant mercy.

God has so many gifts to give the placater child, but he or she must be willing to receive them. Placater children only have to reach out their hands and receive the gifts God and other friends in their lives want to bestow upon them. They need to view themselves in positive ways; they are children of God and worthy of self-respect. God grants them equal status with all of their brothers and sisters in Christ. Placater children deserve equality and they certainly do not need to isolate themselves and draw apart from others by portraying themselves in their own minds as unworthy children.

These are some Scriptures for the placater child:

> *"There is no longer Jew or Greek, there is no longer slave or free, there is no longer male and female; for all of you are one in Christ Jesus."*
>
> *Galatians 3:28 (NRSV)*

> *"Now there are varieties of gifts, but the same Spirit; and there are varieties of services, but the same Lord"*
>
> *1 Corinthians 12:4–5 (NRSV)*

> *"Ask, and it will be given to you; search, and you will find; knock, and the door will be opened to you."*
>
> *Matthew 7:7 (NRSV)*

> *"Humble yourselves before the Lord, and he will exalt you."*
>
> *James 4:10*

> *"Take delight in the Lord, and he will give you the desires of your heart. Commit your way to the Lord; trust in him, and he will act. He will make your vindication shine like the light, and the justice of your cause like the noonday. Be still before the Lord, and wait patiently for him"*
>
> *Psalms 37:4–7*

The Acting-out Child

The acting-out child disrupts family life by providing distractions from the real issues of family addiction. Due to their extremely poor self-image, these children rarely communicate their feelings to adults in a constructive manner. They gravitate toward peers who share common bonds with them, one being low self-esteem. The acting-out children, who are troublemakers in childhood, continue to struggle with conflicts in adulthood. Their negative self-image causes them to characterize themselves as "a nobody." They cannot interact with others in constructive ways and cannot even begin to express their true needs and concerns. Anger and resentment become the only true emotions they seem able to project to the world. Other emotions remain hidden inside the child. On the positive side, these children are creative, have a sense of humor, can exhibit great honesty, and have to ability to lead. However, their gifts are often untapped due to social problems that begin at an early age.[6]

The pastors, church members, or friends of acting-out children must work diligently to find outlets for these children to express their creative gifts in ways that do not hurt others. These children need to encounter church members who become role models. These individuals must exhibit patience and needed discipline. Trusted friends can help these children open up and express their pent-up emotions and bring to the surface their past hurts and resentments that have festered for years.

Acting-out children must, first and foremost, accept God's forgiveness for any wrongdoing in their lives. God erases past mistakes and accepts these children just as they are. He views them as valuable children of God. Their unique gifts are useful for the purpose of building up the kingdom of God, not tearing it down. Acting-out children often express their anger and resentment toward others that grows from own increased sense of neglect and rejection by people in their childhood. Giving this anger over to God will free acting-out children to move forward in their spiritual journey with Him. Harboring anger keeps them as prisoners bound to the destructive forces of addiction. Only God can set them free. God wants what is best for His children who are created in His very image. How He yearns to offer them the gifts of healing and wholeness, if only acting-out children would accept these gifts and use them to help them move forward with hope.

Receive these Scriptures for the acting-out child:

> *"As far as the east is from the west, so far he removes our transgressions from us."*
>
> *Psalms 103:12 (NRSV)*

> *"Rid yourselves, therefore, of all malice, and all guile, insincerity, envy, and all slander."*
>
> *1I Peter 2:1 (NRSV)*

> *"Be angry, but do not sin; do not let the sun go down on your anger, and do not make room for the devil."*
>
> *Ephesians 4:26–27 (NRSV)*

> *"Let us pursue what makes for peace and for mutual edification."*
>
> *Romans 14:19 (NRSV)*

> *"Do not fear, for I am with you; do not be afraid, for I am your God. I will strengthen you, I will help you, I will uphold you with my victorious right hand."*
>
> *Isaiah 41:10 (NRSV)*

The roles that children adopt in the family dynamics of addiction have a huge bearing on their adult lives. They influence not only the day-to-day interaction of these children with others, but also their relationship with God. God wants all of the children of addicts to become whole and healthy persons. This happens only when these children are willing to turn their lives and wills over to God and let Him take control. Prior to doing this, their lives have spun out of control. Trust is an ongoing issue for children of addicts. Before these children can trust others, they must learn to trust God to meet their daily needs. They must accept in faith the assurance that God walks with them at all times and in all places. God can replace the denial and anxiety to which children of addicts cling and sometimes refuse to give over to Him. He can remove their fears and erase their doubts by providing them guidance, strength, and peace.

Opening up to God's dependable and trustworthy presence provides the children of addicts a pattern they can repeat when relating to others. They learn from God's nature that they can trust others and depend on others in their time of need. The common avoidance of feelings children of addicts possess can only be overcome with the dignity and self-worth that God brings to each child. Children of addicts judge themselves (and sometimes others) without mercy. Often unrelenting in their criticism of self, they easily find fault with the slightest mistake. The good news is that God never judges them, but comes to them to bring forgiveness. With God's help and with the reliable help of trusted friends, children of addicts can walk out of the darkness into the light of His love and grace. All they have to do is ask and accept.

We began our chapter with the story of an unforgiving curse placed upon a son by his father. Children of addicts can relate to Ham because they understand what it is like to be cursed in life. Many of them live out shattered lives from constantly having to endure the curse addiction placed upon them. Some of these children received a literal curse from an addictive parent, in the form of angry words and vicious threats that caused deep wounds and lasting hurts that have never healed. Others battled the unrelenting curses of guilt and embarrassment; this sort of grip on a child's life can became so strong that it totally diminishes the self-worth of the child. For children of addicts, God has removed the curse of addiction forever. He has replaced this curse with an eternal blessing. Therefore, these valuable individuals are no longer cursed children of addiction; rather, they are beloved children of God.

Recommended Books for Younger Children of Addicts

An Elephant in the Living Room: The Children's Book, Jill M. Hastings, MD and Marion H. Typpo, PhD, Hazelden, 1984.

Dear Kids of Alcoholics, Lindsey All and Leig Conn, Gurze Books, 1993.

I Wish Daddy Didn't Drink so Much, Judith Vigna, Albert Whitman and Co., 1993.

It Will Never Happen to Me: Growing Up with Addiction as Youngsters, Adolescents, and Young Adults, Claudia Black, Hazelden, 2002.

Kid's Power: Healing Games for Children of Alcoholics, Jerry Moe and Don Pohlmna, HCI, 1989.

My Dad Loves Me, My Dad Has a Disease: A Child's View: Living with Addiction, Claudia Black, MAC Publishing, 1979.

The Addiction Monster and the Square Cat, Sheryl Letzgus McGinnish, Dadivan Books, 2008.

Understanding Addiction and Recovery Through a Child's Eyes: Hope, Help and Healing for Families, M. A. Moe, HCI, 2007.

When a Family Is in Trouble: Children Can Cope with Grief from Drug and Alcohol Addiction, Marge Heegaard, Woodland Press, 1993.

Recommended Books for Adult Children of Addicts

A Guide for Adult Children of Alcoholics, Herbert L. Gravitz and Julie D. Bowden, Simon and Schuster, 1985.

Adult Children of Alchoholics, Jane Geringer Woititz, EdD, Health Communications, Inc., 1983.

Children of Alcoholics: A Guidebook for Educators, Therapists, and Parents, R. J. Ackerman, Learning Publications, 1983.

It Will Never Happen to Me: Growing Up with Addiction, Claudia Black, MACPublishing, Inc., 2001.

Perfect Daughters, Robert Ackerman, Health Communications, 1989.

Safe Passage, Recovery for Adult Children of Alcoholics, Stephanie Brow, John Wiley and Sons, 1991.

Silent Sons, Robert Ackerman, Simon and Schuster, 1993.

The Complete ACOA Sourcebook: Adult Children of Alcoholics at Home, in Work, and in Love, Janet Geringer Woititz, EdD, Health Communications, Inc., 2002.

The Secret Everyone Knows, C. Brooks, The Kroc Foundation, 1981.

Endnotes

1. Peter Steinglass, MD, *The Alcoholic Family* (New York: BasicBooks, 1987), 3–4.

2. *Black, Claudia, It Will Never Happen to Me: Growing Up With Addiction* (Bainbridge Island: MacPublishing, Inc., 2001), 20–23, 55–58.

3. Ibid., 23–25, 59–60.

4. Ibid., 61.

5. Ibid., 26–28, 62–63.

6. Ibid., 29–31, 66–67.

CHAPTER SIX:

When the Addict Is Your Spouse

"Wives, be subject to your husband, as is fitting in the Lord. Husbands, love your wives and never treat them harshly."

Colossians 3:18–19 (NRSV)

In these verses of Scripture, the apostle Paul set forth rules for living in marriage relationships within households of faith. His fervent desire was to bring some order and guidance to the home so that the marriage bond might remain secure. Unfortunately, some of us in modern society have been so offended by what we have perceived as his chauvinistic approach to marriage that we have turned our backs on any teaching of Paul's about marriage. In doing so, we have failed to comprehend the value of what Paul was trying to teach us. Many of us read this passage remembering Paul's words to the married couples at the church at Ephesus:

"Wives, be subject to your husbands as you are to the Lord. for the husband is the head of the wife just as Christ is the head of the church, the body of which he is the Savior."

Ephesians 5:22–23 (NRSV)

Married couples, at least the wife, might be relieved to know that the word "subject" in our text and also in the Ephesians passage does not in way equate subjection with blind obedience. Furthermore, the word "head" in Ephesians actually means "source of life" or "priority," not "authority," as we often mistakenly translate this word. Paul advocated for mutual submission, which is always voluntary, and he only used the word to describe the responsibility of people in Christ, those who have entered into an agreed upon relationship with one another.[1]

Paul reminded us that in the marriage relationship, the husband has an obligation to place a high priority upon the marriage relationship. He is to become to his wife a source of life, loving her like he does his own body and nourishing and tenderly caring for her like Christ does for the church.

> *"In the same way, husbands should love their wives as they do their own bodies. He who loves his wife loves himself. For no one ever hates his own body, but he nourishes and tenderly cares for it, just as Christ does for the church."*
>
> Ephesians 5:28–29 (NRSV)

In a society in which women were given few rights and could rarely support themselves financially, Paul placed upon the wife the obligation to be subject to her husband as is "fitting in the Lord." *As is fitting in the Lord* is meant to explain that there is a limitation to the application of the idea of submission. Yet, if a husband loved his wife and sacrificed for her as Christ does for the church, then surely the woman can subject herself to her husband at the appropriate times in the marriage. The wife is not without obligations, just as the husband is not without responsibilities. For those of us who view marriage as a partnership, Paul called us to submit to one another out of love for Christ and our partner.[2]

It is important to keep this picture before us. We are provided the pattern, according to the Scriptures, of how an ideal marriage works. The ingredients of a strong marriage—love, respect, and trust—must remain always in front of us as we address the faith issues that people married to addicts encounter. These spouses would tell us that they long for marriages of mutual support and submission. Rarely do these kinds of marriages exist once addiction has entered into the marriage relationship. Addiction ruins trust and integrity. The addict traded in the trust and integrity that may once have been a part of the marriage, swapping them for lies and deceit. Rather than the marriage partner being first, the addiction takes first place, thereby relegating the spouse to an inferior role. Promises made on the wedding day are easily broken. Addiction offered the addict the unfulfilled promise of security and the shallow promise of relief from the problems of life. The addict believed addiction's shallow promises, putting them above the strong promises of the marriage covenant.

Furthermore, if we took Paul's writings on marriage and interpreted these teachings as some have, we could easily justify instructing people to stay in marriages even when they are placed in grave danger. Innocent victims in marriages where addiction is present might feel compelled to remain in an unsafe relationship. If a wife believed that the Bible teaches her that her husband ruled over her as head of the house and she is subjected to him without any rights or any opinions, she could very well be convinced that her faith requires her to stay loyal to her husband even in cases of abuse or infidelity.

As people of faith, we define marriage as a covenant. Our marriage covenant contains the promises we made to one another at our wedding ceremonies. Our wedding vows were voiced in the presence of God and witnessed by our family and friends. Many of our ceremonies took place in a church sanctuary, a place we considered holy space, and were officiated over by a minister authorized by the church to administer these sacred vows. Solemn vows and cherished moments of promise have been shattered by the unholy and dishonest actions that addiction brings to a marriage.

Spouses of addicts now wonder if their vows have been obliterated by the actions of their addicted partners. Husbands or wives promised to love, honor, and cherish one another until they were parted by death. It would not take death, however; addiction wedged itself between these partners, effectively casting a divisive shadow upon their homes. Some have painfully discovered that their spouses loved and cherished his or her addiction with a passion, so the other partners are forced to take second place. Their spouses vowed to be faithful to their marriage covenant, which included sexual fidelity. Perhaps he or she now spends hours downloading pornography. A sexual addiction may have driven some spouses to seek out illicit sexual relationships outside of the marriage covenant. For some, their spouse's alcohol or drug addiction erased the times of intimacy; instead the non-addicted spouse spends worrisome nights alone. A partner's gambling addiction can easily plunge a family into debt. The costs are not just monetary; trust is also a precious commodity that is gambled away. The harm inflicted leads many individuals facing uncertainly to question whether their families or marriages will ever recover. All of these are ways in which addiction has forced its unwelcome presence into the center of family life and attempted to destroy sacred marriage covenants.

We must not forget the other side of the marriage covenant, however. Not only have marriage partners promised to love, honor, and cherish each other reciprocally, they also agreed to support each other in the myriad situations that life brought their way. These times included "in sickness and health, for better or for worse." Spouses of addicts must give themselves a great deal of credit for fulfilling these vows and living day by day with the challenging ordeals addiction has brought to a marriage. Some have been faithful to a spouse who was sickened with the disease of addiction. Others have supported a spouse who has broken the marriage vows again and again. Spouses of addicts have extended God-like love and grace to a person who has not fulfilled his or her part of the covenant. They have kept their end of the covenant agreement, even when their spouse has violated his or her part.

We are reminded of the ways in which God covenanted with his children in the past and continues to covenant with us today. A biblical covenant is intended to be binding on both parties involved, that is, God and humankind. Yet, every time God made a covenant with humankind in the Bible, humanity quickly turned around and selfishly broke the covenant. However, God remained faithful and forgave this unruly creation. Time and again, God renewed the covenant drawing people back to Him with tender cords of love and grace.

In the same way, spouses of addicts have remained faithful to their addicted spouses. Some have done so in spite of ridicule, criticism, and humiliation. I wanted to assure faithful spouses that their marriage covenants remained honorable, even if the actions of their addicted spouse seemed to indicate otherwise. Every time a faithful partner extends forgiveness to an unworthy spouse, this forgiving spouse acted with God-like love, grace, and patience. The unfaithful spouse was not deserving of mercy, but they were shown this grace out of respect for the fidelity of the marriage covenant.

These words of affirmation were not intended in any way to dishonor those who have been forced to make the devastating decision to end their marriages or for those who have chosen to remove their spouse from their home due to his or her addiction. Some spouses were abused physically, emotionally, and mentally. No spouses of addicts should ever be required to live in fear for their safety or the safety of their children. As parents, we were chosen and obligated by God to offer protection for our children and ourselves. The marriage covenant was upheld and respected as long as it was possible to maintain. Some people stayed in unsafe situations much longer than was wise. Others are addicts themselves. Still others are children of addicts who repeated the patterns of addiction they experienced in their own family life by marrying addicts.

Whatever the marital situation, these individuals must not place guilt upon themselves just because I offered affirmation to other spouses of addicts for their continued fulfillment of their marriage covenants. These others also acted with courage in the face of addiction. Each person comes to addiction from a unique background and different marital situation. Each individual must decide for him- or herself how he or she will handle the marriage when thrust into the chaos of addiction.

I recognize that some people obligatorily remained in their marriage covenants, perhaps primarily for practical reasons. They may not have given a shred of thought to the theological basis behind covenants in their faith and in their marriage, especially how these might be connected to one another. They have stayed in the marriage because of financial needs or for the sake of their children. However, I do believe that eventually the spouses of addicts must consider the meaning of their marriage vows with the understanding that it is a *covenant relationship*. The marriage covenant is representative of the covenant God made with humanity. So when marriage covenants are broken and when we find our spouses to be undependable, our faith is greatly affected. Perhaps we questioned whether God is dependable and forgiving or whether God—like our unfaithful spouses—had also turned into a covenant-breaker.

Scripture assures us that we serve a God who is dependable and that the covenant God established with each of us can never be broken. The prophet Jeremiah spoke of an everlasting covenant that God made and a covenant that God would never rescind:

> *"I will make an everlasting covenant with them,*
> *never to draw back from doing good to them... "*
>
> *Jeremiah 32:40a (NRSV)*

Our God is dependable even when our marriage partners are undependable. God never withdraws His everlasting, faithful covenant with us, even when our marriage covenants are destroyed by the unfaithful actions of an addicted spouse who may continue to withdraw from an intimate relationship with us. God's trustworthy promises are proven to be true over and over again, even if the promises of our spouses turned out to be false.

Many of our marital situations can never improve unless our spouse makes the decision to seek help by finally entering treatment and embracing recovery. Perhaps some are not to this point in their marriage yet. However, know that even in the unfaithful covenant of a marriage threatened and destroyed by addiction, God comes as a faithful partner. God never forsook us for one moment, even if our spouses abandoned us for alcohol, drugs, pornography, sexual addiction, eating disorders, or a combination of these diseases.

The prophet Isaiah spoke comforting words to his people when they faced innumerable uncertainties of the future because their homeland had been invaded and they had been exiled to a foreign land. They existed day after day with the constant fear of an unknown world where they thought perhaps God had abandoned them. Spouses of addicts also find themselves, like the people of Isaiah's time, fearful and unsure of what the future holds for their marriages. It is as if they have been exiled from their marriages by a force far beyond their control, a force that sought to wreak only havoc and chaos on their marriages. These words of Isaiah, given to his suffering people, are words that the spouses of addicts need to hear with clarity as they suffer with marriages torn apart by addiction:

> *"Do not fear, for I am with you; do not be afraid, for I am your God; I will strengthen you, I will help you, I will uphold you with my victorious right hand."*
>
> *Isaiah 41:10 (NRSV)*

> *"For I, the Lord your God, hold your right hand; it is I who say to you, 'So do not fear, I will help you.'"*
>
> *Isaiah 41:13 (NRSV)*

Marriage covenants are bound up in trust. For the spouses of addicts, this trust was broken over and over again. Many families of addicts deal with the issues of trust, and it weighs heavily upon their faith in God. Yet, I believe that the spouses of addicts in particular have a difficult time with the issue of trust because it is so pivotal to the marriage relationship.

We expect our spouses to be honest with us, but we have been lied to repeatedly. The basis of our marriage was founded on integrity and trust, and when these virtues are absent from a marriage, it makes it difficult, in turn, to trust others and God.

Just as I have advised families of addicts to seek out trustworthy people in whom to confide, I would suggest to spouses of addicts that they also find a trusted friend. This person may be a pastor, a friend in his or her community of faith, an acquaintance, or a relative. Spouses of addicts need someone with whom they can talk about the problems they are facing, someone who offers understanding and empathy. Support groups are available in the community and are filled with people who share our story of addiction. Seek out these support groups and attend them regularly; these friends offer the assurance that the spouses of addicts are not forced to walk alone in their addiction journeys.

Addiction tends to be a disease of isolation. This holds particularly true for spouses of addicts, especially those who encounter the joint duties of caring for an addicted spouse and children in the family. Their time is consumed with facing the problems of addiction and, at the same time, attempting to provide an atmosphere of normalcy in family life, which is an almost impossible task when dealing with addiction. However, even when the spouse of an addict does not have children to consume his or her time and attention, he or she can still end up in lonely places because of addiction. Once people enter into a marriage relationship, we assume that these individuals desire and need intimacy and time alone to strengthen and develop their marriage. We often do not wish to interfere or impose upon the marriage relationship, so sometimes spouses of addicts get ignored in our attempts to allow privacy in the marriage.

As friends and pastors of spouses of addicts, we must exhibit sensitivity toward these hurting people. We must grant them opportunities to open up to us honestly and without judgment. We must listen compassionately to what they share with us and give them helpful advice on ways to enter recovery groups that offer help for both for the addict and for the spouse. Remember, the spouse of an addict has put him- or herself in a vulnerable position by talking and sharing with others. They have shared their family secrets, hoping these will be kept in the strictest confidence. We must be careful not to violate the trust they have placed in us. We must do all in our power to support and nurture them toward recovery.

Trust becomes an issue for the spouses of addicts, not just in relationships with others but also in their relationships with God. How can people who have trusted in a marriage that they thought was God-ordained turn around and trust in God now that their marriages are in shambles? Was it not God who guided them to find one another in the first place and then led them to establish a relationship with one another? Was God not present to witness their marriage vows just as their friends and family were? Did He not bless their union when they stood together and took their marriage vows? These are all valid questions that spouses of addicts ask God. If they are people of faith, they earnestly believed that God brought them together as a couple, was present at their marriage ceremonies, and blessed their marriages.

People of faith must earnestly believe that God led us to our spouses and blessed our marriages with God's abiding presence. However, this does not mean God did not grant our addicts free will to make choices that would sever our marriage relationships. God now works in partnership with us to try and restore the broken pieces of our marriages. God cannot do this if our spouses are unwilling to cooperate and get the help they so desperately need.

As people of faith, we must place our whole trust in God. God does not desire our partial trust, but our ultimate loyalty. The Scriptures assure us that we can trust God due to His dependable nature. Trust flows from the examples we have observed of the times and ways people have proven themselves to be trustworthy. The same is true with God. Our trust is gained when we see God at work in the world, bringing healing and restoration to hurt persons. God wants to take our hurts and transform them into wholeness. God has proven many times that He can be trusted. Just as God gives us His full attention at all times in our faith journey, we must pledge full loyalty to Him.

God wants each of us to have strong, vibrant marriages. Genesis 2:24 tells us that in marriage, "a man will leave his father and mother and be united ot his wife, and they will become one flesh." Jesus instructs the people in Matthew 19:8 that Moses allows divorce due to the hardness of a person's heart, that is problems that enter the marriage that partners cannot resolve. Jesus desires couples to pledge loyalty to one another in marriage. The disease of addiction works to destroy even the strongest of marriages, turning them from healthy relationships to unhealthy ones. We must remember that God cannot be blamed for our failed marriages and that He certainly did not cause our spouse's disease. We must not blame ourselves or place guilt upon our heads for something we could not control. What we cannot control, God can. When we turn our marriages over to

Him, we admit that we do not have the power to control our addicts or our marriages. We place our marriage in God's hands so that we can gain sanity in our own lives. Our recovery is not dependent on whether our marriages improve or our addicts change; our recovery revolves around our willingness to make the necessary changes to start ourselves on the path to sobriety.

Turning our lives and our spouses over to God never proves to be easy, but we must do it in order to have any sanity in our own lives. When we give up control, we allow God to begin to work. Our freedom from addiction begins the moment we let Him take control of our addict. We then start to work our own program of recovery, even if our addict never joins us.

It takes great courage to tell an addicted spouse that we refuse to put up with his or her excessive dependency or childlike behavior any longer. We have already discovered that our addicted spouses have a difficult time making decisions. Avoiding responsibility and decision-making has caused our addicts to depend upon us to make all of the important decisions in the family. When we turn our addicts over to God, we need to let our addict know that he or she must begin to make his or her own decisions.

Addicts typically have low self-esteem. When we continually criticize or ridicule addicts in our lives, we will only reinforce this negative self-image. Spouses of addicts can also be drawn into thinking less of themselves and belittling themselves for things over which they have little control. We are children of God, created in God's very image. God never wants us to wallow in self-pity or blame. Keeping a positive self-image as beloved children of God helps spouses of addicts face each day in addiction believing in their self-worth. They are called by God to live with dignity and take pride in themselves, despite their external circumstances.

Addicts tend to isolate themselves from others, especially as their disease progresses. Addicted spouses may seek to keep us from our support network of friends and church members. The partners of addicts must be especially careful about isolating themselves from others; they must continue to reach out in friendship to others, especially in their faith communities. Keeping a connection with the church and maintaining close friendships among church friends increases their chances of continual growth in the faith.

The partner of an addicted spouse must realize that this spouse is likely to exhibit emotional immaturity while in addiction. A forty-year-old man or woman can act like an immature seventeen-year-old child. We have to take care of this "child," who adds an additional burden to our already hectic lifestyles. Also, we may have observed that our addicts exhibit difficulties with expressing emotions. When this happens in marriages, couples drift apart over time because they are unable to share with one another; they become unable to communicate their true feelings.

Couples must confront two other issues common to all addictive households, yet especially prevalent in the marriage relationship. These are the issues of manipulation and enabling, both powerful tools our addicts will use effectively to weaken our will power. Addicts quickly learn how to manipulate others, especially those closest to them. These loved ones constantly demonstrate their concern for the well-being of the addict. Spouses of addicts are easy prey for manipulation; too often they become a willing victim as enablers. Partners of addicts get caught in the trap of manipulation because they love their spouse, wish to please their spouse, and find it extremely difficult to turn down the spouse's requests. The disease of addiction distorts our spouses into selfish individuals who want immediate gratification. They will beg and plead, often like little children, until they wear down our defenses and we give in to their demands.

Strong marriages are built on the ability of both partners to satisfy the needs of one another, based on mutual respect. The partners of addicts learn that their needs are unimportant in the marriage. The addict's needs take priority. Those married to addicts frequently allow this to happen through their own actions of enabling. Addicts are so good at manipulating that they convince us we must cast aside our own valid concerns in deference to their selfish desires.

The spouses of addicts wear down emotionally, physically, and in particular spiritually when they constantly provide non-stop care for another person. If they are not careful, they begin to distance themselves from God, from the very source that can provide them strength and give them discernment. They can also easily cut themselves off from their faith friends, who could offer guidance and direction on what to do about enabling. Even when spouses allow friends to offer suggestions, the addict can counteract with such forceful manipulation that his or her spouse silences the wisdom of friends, turns a deaf ear to sound advice, and continues to enable the addict.

We enable our addict out of our love for him or her, even when it makes little sense. We reason that we are fulfilling our marriage vows when we act out of love, even when in the back of our minds, we know what we are doing is wrong. Often our addicted spouses will convince us that our enabling and their manipulation makes perfect sense. We want to please our spouse. If we examine the situation, some of us take pleasure in our enabling because of our instincts to protect or nurture our spouses.

A wife may hope to entice her husband away from alcohol by pouring out his liquor bottle and tucking him into bed, because her maternal instincts are satisfied in the process. What she discovers is that her husband will only go out and purchase another bottle. An alcoholic husband may manipulate his wife and convince her to drive him to the liquor store. He tells her that she would not want to see him suffer the symptoms of withdrawal from alcohol. A husband may continue to give his wife money for drugs or gambling because he has always provided for his wife's financial needs and he cannot stand to see her unhappy. His head tells him that what he is doing is wrong, but his heart tells him that a part of his husbandly role is to please his wife. A husband with a sexual addiction may heap guilt upon his wife when he blames her for failing to fulfill him sexually.

We engage in unreasonable behavior when we continue to enable our addicted spouses and when we constantly allow our addicts to manipulate us. God's intent was for the marriage relationship to be one of equality and partnership based on love, honor, and respect. This cannot happen in our current marriage relationships until our addicts enter recovery. However, this does not mean we must remain a hostage in our own marriages. God invites us to freedom from enabling and manipulation, regardless of what our addicts decide. God wants us to take necessary steps to set ourselves free by stopping our enabling and saying no to our spouse's manipulative requests. This will not be easy; it will be one of the hardest tasks we will encounter in our marriage to an addict. Our addicted spouse will use all of his or her persuasive powers to blame us and make us feel guilty for our shortcomings. He or she will cry out that we have forsaken our marriage vows and do not love him or her anymore. Do not buy into this type of childish behavior any longer. We must fervently pray and ask God to free us from the slavery of manipulation and enabling that are characteristic of an addictive marriage.

> *"For freedom Christ has set us free. Stand firm, therefore, and do not submit again to a yoke of slavery."*
>
> *Galatians 5:1 (NRSV)*

Sometimes enabling and manipulation lead the spouse of an addict into dangerous situations. For instance, if the spouse of an abusive addict calls the police, yet fails to press charges, the addict faces few, if any, consequences for his or her actions. Perhaps the addict manipulates the spouse with promises that he or she will change or will seek help. Or perhaps he or she lays a guilt trip upon the spouse by using genuine feelings of love for manipulative purposes. The addict will convince the spouse that if he or she truly loved the addict, the spouse would not have the addict arrested. Later on, the abuse may escalate as the promises become lies and the manipulation continues in the marriage. The cycle of enabling kicks back in, and the abused spouse remains in a violent marriage.

Never continue to live in a home with an abusive spouse. God never intends for any of us to abide in a dangerous situation or to put our children in harm's way. It is necessary to get our children and us out of an abusive home and if necessary seek legal help. Do not hesitate to call the police to intervene if their help is required. We must not be afraid to press charges when necessary to provide safety for our children and ourselves. Children are a gift from God, and God has given parents the role of caregivers. God calls us to protect our children above our marriages when physical abuse is being inflicted upon our children or us. Finding safety for our children and seeking our own safety does not in any way violate our marriage vows. Abusive spouses must be held accountable for any acts of violence toward family members. God stands on the side of justice, desiring wholeness for all people, and always defending those who are helpless. The psalmist spoke of a God of justice:

> *"He loves righteousness and justice. The earth is full*
> *of the steadfast love of the Lord."*
>
> *Psalms 33:5 (NRSV)*

Ask God to give guidance on how to help your addicted spouse find just the right recovery community. In recovery, he or she will begin to deal with the problems addicts have of expressing emotions and learn how to act more like a responsible adult. Be patient, because your spouse will need time to undo negative behavior patterns by turning them around into positive actions. Be aware that even in recovery, spouses may fall back into addictive behavior habits from time to time.

Turning their will to God is a very important step for many addicts on the path to recovery. In a recovery program, our spouse will declare that his or her life has become unmanageable and totally out of control. Spouses of addicts must profess the same admission if they want to get better. Our addicts are not the only ones affected by the disease of addiction. We, as their family members, are greatly affected as well. This disease has turned our lives and marriages upside down. When we turn the disease over to God and declare that our lives are unmanageable, we give God power to take away the destructive power of this disease. Only God can restore stability in our lives, because without God's help, this disease manifests itself in evil, destructive ways. God works for our good, but the disease of addiction only seeks to tear down our marriages and manipulate us into thinking there is little hope to be found.

When your partner enters a recovery program, be as supportive as possible. Understand that he or she must be connected with a support group. Spouses need to attend support meetings regularly. In early sobriety, addicts are encouraged to attend meetings daily. These meetings will cut into our family time, and we may begin to feel some jealousy toward our spouses' recovery programs. The recovery program must be a priority for our addicted spouses. I know what many are thinking: *I have sacrificed so much in our marriage, so why is my marriage not a priority?* Recovery is a lifelong journey. Not supporting our spouse in his or her recovery attempts can cause conflict in our marriage and force our spouse to choose between his or her recovery program or us. This is an unfair choice for anyone to have to make. True understanding goes a long way toward helping our spouses in their recovery efforts. Seeking and receiving help is not easy; it takes great courage and determination.

There are also meetings in the community that spouses of addicts can attend, to offer support to families of addicts. It can be beneficial for spouses of addicts to schedule their meetings on the same day and time as their addicts, if possible, to keep partners from being absent from home several nights a week. Children can be cared for by loving grandparents or trusted friends. There are even some meetings that allow children to be present. Older children may attend Al-anon meetings that take place at the same time and place as the AA meetings. We should attend these meetings even if our addict is not in a recovery program, however. The meetings are designed to help the spouses of addicts with their recovery. Most of these meetings have a spiritual dimension. These groups will connect us with the spouses of other addicts, many of whom understand our frustrations. The recovery groups for spouses of addicts encourage them to let go of the addict, placing him or her under God's guidance. Various topics are discussed, especially the subject of enabling. Participants are led to understand the dangers of enabling and other unhealthy patterns in family life.

If spouses of addicts have children living in the home, these spouses shoulder the additional burden of trying to care for an addict and their children as well. They must work extra hard to create an environment where children have some sense of stability. When spouses focus all of their attention on addicted partners, the children are often neglected and may harbor resentment toward us. Addiction creates chaos and inconsistency in home life. It is important to help children understand that addiction is a disease. Assure them that they did nothing to cause the disease. Talk with them about faith matters. Tell them that God loves them, and let them know that God also loves the mother or father who is an addict. Help them to understand that God did not cause the disease to bring punishment to the addict or to the family.

Enter into prayer with children, asking God to help the addicted parent and strengthen the entire family. Read books together about addiction. Seek help from friends and church members in caring for children. Encourage teenage children to attend community support groups, and seek professional help for children if they are having difficulties coping with addiction issues. If spouses enter treatment, go together for allowed visits as a family and encourage the partner's recovery efforts in front of children in the family.

The spouses of addicts often ask: "What did I do to deserve this in my marriage?" We did nothing to deserve addiction, and neither did our spouses. If our spouse was dying of cancer, we would not hold him or her responsible for the illness, and we would not place blame upon ourselves either. Rather, we would do everything in our power to seek healing. Like cancer or any other life-threatening disease, addiction renders our beloved spouses powerless and vulnerable. The effect of addiction quickly spreads to all family members to catch. Before it spreads totally out of control, however, the spouses of addicts must intervene and do all they can to get help. Even if our spouse refuses the help offered to him or her, the non-addicted partner must reach out and grab all of the resources available.

The disease of addiction inflicted upon any marriage can swiftly destroy the trust that individuals placed in their partners on the day they stood together and recited their marriage vows. Only recovery for us and for our addicted partners—if they will agree to get help—can make the difference in restoring fragmented marriages. What is "fitting in the Lord," as far as God is concerned, is that spouses join together to become whole and healthy people. Then, united as one, they can rebuild their marriage on the promises made at their wedding ceremonies. Take time to remember the holy and sacred promises made to each other as partners in the marriage covenant. Let these vows, along with God's grace and love, be the guiding lights that lead us out of the darkness of addiction and into the hope of new promises.

Recommended Books for Spouses of Addicts

Bought Out & Spent! Recovery from Compulsive Shopping & Spending, Terrence Daryl Shulman, Infinity Publishing, 2008.

Confronting Your Spouse's Pornography Problem, Rory C. Reid and Dan Gray, Silverleaf Press, 2006.

Don't Call It Love: Recovery from Sexual Addictions by Patrick Carnes, Bantam, 1992.

False Intimacy: Understanding the Struggle of Sexual Addiction, Harry W. Schaumburg, NavPress Publishing Group, 1997.

Food Addiction: The Body Knows, Kay Sheppard, HCI, 1993.

Hope After Betrayal: Healing When Sexual Addiction Invades Your Marriage, Meg Wilson, Kregel Publications, 2007.

I Surrender All: Rebuilding a Marriage Broken by Pornography, Clay and Renee Cross and Mark A. Tabb, NavPress Publishing Group, 2005.

Love, Infidelity & Sexual Addiction: A Codependent's Perspective, Cristine A. Adams, Authors Choice Press, 2001.

Marriage on the Rocks: Learning to Live with Yourself and an Alcoholic, Janet Geringer Woititz, EdD, Health Communications, 1979.

My Secret Life with a Sex Addict: From Discovery to Recovery, Emma Dawson, Thornton Publishing, 2004.

Endnotes

1. *Women in the Bible*, Mary J. Evans, (Downers Grove: InterVarsity Press, 1983), 77.

2. Ibid., 73–76.

CHAPTER SEVEN:

When the Addict Is Your Child

"When Israel was a child, I loved him, and out of Egypt I called my son. The more I called them, the more they went from me; they kept sacrificing to the Baals, and offering incense to idols. Yet it was I who taught Ephraim to walk, I took them up in my arms; but they did not know that I healed them. I led them with cords of human kindness, with bands of love. I was to them like those who lift infants to their cheeks. I bent down to them and fed them. How can I give you up, Ephraim? How can I hand you over, O Israel? How can I make you like Admah? How can I treat you like Zeboiim? My heart recoils within me; my compassion grows warm and tender."

Hosea 11:1–4, 8 (NRSV)

The prophet Hosea provided us with a compassionate portrait of Parent God. God yearned for the allegiance of His wayward child, who flippantly broke the familial covenant by keeping company with pagan gods. God recounted in motherly terms the parenting skills God demonstrated toward the nation of Israel, whose people the prophet depicted as God's son. God taught Ephraim to walk, sheltered Israel in His protective arms, bent down and fed the hungry child, lifted up the infant in a snuggling embrace, and tenderly guided the son with chords and bonds of kindness and love.

God simply cannot give up on the son He has birthed and parented. God inquired with a fervent, passionate, parental cry, "How can I give you up?"

Almost every responsible parent can relate to God's heart-wrenching pain. God's emotional response summed up exactly what many parents in the same situation have uttered. Our answer to the various dilemmas thrust upon us as parents of prodigal children echoes Parent God's final decision toward estranged Israel: "I cannot ever give you up because you are my child and I love you." God welcomed the rebellious son back into the circle of His encompassing love. Acting out of unconditional love, God extends undeserved forgiveness toward an unappreciative Israel. Rather than condemn, God chooses to work tirelessly to restore the broken relationship between parent and child.

Parents of addicts readily identify with Hosea's story of God's unrelenting love for disobedient children who have violated the family covenant of trust. These children have alienated themselves from the family by engaging in behavior that contains no redeeming qualities. In their addictive states, they have manipulated, lied, and dominated the family to the point where parents have come close to breaking down completely. Parents are left totally exhausted, completely frustrated, and utterly puzzled at the ability of addiction to dominate their lives. They are horrified to see their son or daughter changed so completely, caring about little else but feeding their addictions. Yet, parents of addicts continued to support and enable their sons and daughters because they love them and they hold in high regard their responsibility to be good parents. They cannot imagine giving up on their children, just as God could not conceive of letting Israel go without a fight.

Christian parents whose children are addicts can certainly read into the Hosea passage their own experiences of relating to an addicted child. The story of unfaithful Israel has a familiar air about it that rings true for parents of addicts and provides a sense of clarity for them about God's faithful love of their children in spite of their mistakes. Like Israel, their children were attracted and lured by the foreign god. For Israel, the god is Baal; for the children of these parents, the god is addiction. Israel was so mesmerized by the fertility god Baal and so totally addicted to the foreign gods that she was willing to sacrifice God's love in exchange for the addictive habits of pagan worship. For parents of addicts, their sons and daughters have thrown away the nurturing environment of family life to worship at the altar of addiction. Drugs, alcohol, gambling, pornography, and other addictive disorders become the gods to which they bow down to, the gods they now serve with the utmost allegiance. These children, some without a drop of remorse, traded in the love of their parents, their siblings, and their stable home environment for the false promises of the gods of addiction.

Christian parents of addicts often defend their continued role as gullible enablers, constant deniers, and effective blamers, due to their unconditional love for their addict. Addiction almost always demands more and more of parents and the addicts in an attempt to destroy relationships, and try as they may, these parents can never truly offer their children unconditional love because they are not God. Only God can provide addicts with unconditional love. Parents often use the excuse of unconditional love to prevent themselves from having to set consequences for the addict. Setting boundaries for addicts requires *conditional* love.

When speaking of unconditional love, what most parents of addicts are trying to convey is that the love they hold for their children is not dependent on whether the child loves them back or acts responsibly. Parents hate the addiction, but they continue to love the child. Parents abhor the way addiction has turned their children into people they hardly recognize, but they are steadfast in their love of the children they remember before addiction. They recognize that their son or daughter destroyed by addiction does not come close to the child they once knew. These parents carry fond memories—like God in the Hosea passage—of watching their children grow and teaching them important life lessons. Now they recognize the ways in which addiction has turned their family life into a shambles; yet, they refuse to abandon their love for the children God gave them.

Parents demonstrate their sincere desire to rescue their children from all dangerous situations. Parents strive for their children to avoid circumstances that harm them, taking whatever steps are necessary to fulfill their God-given responsibilities to keep their children safe and provide a warm environment. When confronted with the children's addictions, parents heroically attempt to "rescue" their children. Many go out of their way to rearrange their lives to accommodate every need of their addicted children. Parents sacrifice their time, self-care, and family relationships because their addicts are greedy and helpless in their addictive lifestyles. Even if the parents' own lives are turned upside down or put on hold, the needs of the addicts often come first. Parents justify their chaotic, often irrational behavior by telling themselves their addicted children cannot survive without their help.

Most parents form loving bonds with their children the moment they are born or adopted. Children strongly tug at parent's heartstrings, and parents want to spare their children the trials and tribulations that life often brings. Parents know that children cannot avoid problems in life, but they want to shelter their children nevertheless. It is the parental instinct to fight for one's children at all costs. Addiction leaves parents in a risky position. Parents tried to be superhuman, and they are appalled when their rescue efforts do not effect a change in their addicts. They believe their love and devotion to their children is enough to save them. When their efforts fail, they blame themselves, and eventually their feelings of hopelessness cast a dark shadow on their lives.

Denial

Many parents have not even reached the stage described above, however. They are still in denial that the addiction even exists. Parents begin to notice signs of addiction, but these are often ignored or excused for anything else but addiction. Parents do not want their children to become addicts, so they become blinded to the facade put up by their addicted children. Parents have fond childhood memories of their children; thus, they overlook many of the obvious patterns of addiction. They find it difficult to believe their children have become addicts, remembering instead the precious child they brought into the world. They remember with affection all of the hopes and dream they had for that child. Often, by the time parents transition through their denial and admit that they have children who are addicts, the addiction has reached overwhelming proportions, and full-blown addiction has overtaken the lives of these children.

Many parents hide their secret from outsiders when their suspicions about addiction are confirmed. They are fearful that others will judge them as unfit parents or gossip about their family. They may initially be so shocked that they cannot fathom the truth. Their addicts live in a constant state of denial and will lie to their parents to keep from revealing their addictions. Since parents only desire the best for their children, they are drawn into the false hope that perhaps they were mistaken all along and that their children are honest in telling them the truth that they are not addicts, after all.

God wants parents of addicts to know the horrible truth that their children are indeed addicted. God never desired us to stay in darkness and live with lies. Facing our children honestly—but never judgmentally—can allow our sons and daughters to open up and confess. When this happens, when they are totally honest with us, we must not scorn or mock them or vent our anger upon them. We put forth our best efforts when we are able to explain calmly to them of our understanding that addiction is a disease and that we will commit ourselves to doing all in our power to help them get better. Some children may laugh at us or ridicule us, but we must not let their reactions keep us from offering them help. We cannot fix or cure their disease, but we can offer to aid them in the search for professional help that will get them on the path to recovery. We have a God-given responsibility and obligation as parents to do these things to the best of our abilities.

Despite the knowledge that addiction can change our children from honest, kind, and respectable people into conniving individuals who cheat, steal, lie, and manipulate their families, parents still strongly love their children. Sometimes this well-intended love, however, causes parents to refuse to set boundaries and neglect to impose consequences upon the addict. Failure to do so, even when done out of love, can be detrimental to the addict and to the parents.

Christian parents whose children are addicts often grapple with issues of faith. They believe that God gave their children to them as precious gifts and that they claim the responsibility always to love their children, regardless. Some parents are filled with guilt, thinking that perhaps their incompetent parenting skills or lack of parental discipline caused their children to become addicts. They struggle with issues of enabling, denial, and blame, just like all family members of addicts do. Thus, wrestling with these factors impacts their faith, often leading to more questions than answers.

Guilt and Blame

Many parents of addicts must understand that they did nothing to cause their children to become addicts. It was not their lack of parenting skills, it was not their failure at discipline, it was not their divorce, and it was not the lack of quality or quantity time they spent with their children when they were growing up. Parents can spend endless hours second-guessing their actions and decisions. They need to quit blaming themselves, otherwise the guilt can become too great to bear. Addiction reveals itself as a dangerous disease.

There are of course exceptions. For instance, a parent who is himself an addict might have modeled behavior that the child patterned. Or worse yet, an addict parent could give the child addictive substances.

Certainly, some parents are aware of having a family history of addiction. There are parents who admit that they themselves are addicts and spend time cringing with guilt, recognizing they may have passed along the predisposition to addiction to their children. The truth remains that addiction can be passed from generation to generation, but parents should not blame their family history or themselves. Parents who carry a family history of addiction sometimes blame themselves because they trace their child's addiction back to a parent or a family member. While it is true that children of addicts often become addicts themselves and the family genetic factor greatly increases the chances of the inheritance of the disease, families with addiction in their past should not blame themselves. Even in families with a history of addiction, parents cannot always be blamed for the choices children make.

Guilt and blame often prevent parents of addicts and addicts themselves from growing in their relationship with God. God becomes an easy target for their blame. While God entrusts parents with the responsibility to care for their children, He does not expect parents to carry out their tasks alone. God maintains a parenting role as well. Parents may reason that God has abandoned their children to addiction. They may conclude that God has stopped caring about their children, now that they are addicts. God cannot be blamed for the children's addiction. God created these children, and God only wants a fulfilling and purposeful life for each of them, as they are created in His image. God gives each individual the gift of free will. Children make their own decisions to drink, take drugs, gamble, or view pornography. God's all-powerful love and grace for these children never stops, but He refuses to intervene and violate our children's rights to choose for themselves the directions they follow in life. Parents must never blame God or accuse God of turning their children into addicts.

We serve a God who cries with the son who drinks himself into oblivion. We worship a God who never forsakes the daughter when she sticks a needle into her arm. We show allegiance to a God who walks beside our addicted children each step of the way on their addiction journeys. God never forsakes our children for one moment, even when these children refuse to acknowledge God's presence and reject His grace. Parents must not blame God; rather they must believe that He is an abiding presence for their children.

All these sons or daughters have to do is reach out to God and let Him take control of their downhill-spiraling, out-of-control lives. When we blame our addicted children for a disease that they cannot control, parents add to their children's mounting guilt. Addicts often carry around huge amounts of guilt that continue with them even when they are in recovery. When parents constantly belittle addicts with accusations and blame them for past mistakes, relationships between children and their parents are severed. This can also undermine both the parents' and their children's relationships with God. Children whose parents consistently hurl insults at them for their addiction troubles diminish these children's self-worth. These addicts, filled with guilt, transfer this guilt to their relationship with God, thinking they are unworthy to approach God. After all, if the people who are called by God to care for them deem them unworthy, perhaps God also declares them unredeemable. Parent accusations play a role in the children's perceptions that God judges them harshly. Addicted children's self-imposed guilt and blame will be enough baggage to last them for a lifetime. Parents need not and must not add to this guilt.

When parents blame themselves for their child's addiction, they also hinder their own relationship with God. The guilt that constantly dwells in their background not only adds stress to their already chaotic lives, but it affects their spiritual lives as well. They begin to notice changes in the quality and quantity of their prayer life, their devotional time, and their growth in their faith. Letting go of the guilt and blame frees us to trust God in the areas of our lives that we cannot control. No parent can control addiction. It is a far greater force of evil than parents ever imagined, and even attempting to fight it exhausts their physical and mental resources. Parents must relinquish their guilt to God, who absolves them of any blame for the addiction of their children.

Forgiveness

Parents must go one step further. Not only must they hand their guilt and blame over to God, but they must also offer forgiveness to their children. *Forget that,* parents may be thinking. This is the son or daughter who stole from them, deceived them, caused upheaval in their family, and made life miserable for them. They cannot even conceive of offering their child any fragment of forgiveness. However, if parents are ever going to get well themselves, they must extend forgiveness to their children. Parents must remember that they are not exempt from addiction. Addiction affects all members of the family, not just the addict. Family members are not exempt from the effects of addiction.

Offering forgiveness to their addicted children does not mean that parents condone their addictive behaviors. When they reach out with forgiveness, they allow God's healing powers to begin to flow into their lives and the lives of their children. God does not ask parents to excuse all of the addictive behaviors that cause their children to act harshly. God never expects parents to forget all of the heartbreaks they experience as a result of their child's addiction. God is the only one who can forget and wipe the slate clean for their addicted children. Parents must let God clean that slate. The parents' concern revolves around offering forgiveness for their children, a move that ultimately frees parents to begin their own plans for their recovery.

Enabling

As parents of addicts work to remove guilt and blame from their lives, they must also address the issue of enabling. When parents enable, they begin to recognize their habits of helping their child are actually hindering the addicted child's ability to change. This causes the parents a great deal of guilt. They tell themselves they cannot stop enabling because it is their parental responsibility to care for their children at all costs. Then, if parents do eventually stop enabling, they are guilt-ridden because they have broken the ties of dependence that bind them to their children. Letting go of the children parents have brought into the world and nurtured through their lives is not easy. Seeing children suffer when they refuse to get help and continue to live addictive lives breaks our hearts. Ironically, parents are caught in the traps of guilt and blame, regardless of whether they enable or whether they stop.

Both enabling and the decision to stop enabling become faith issues for parents of addicts. When they enable, parents give children their blessings to avoid their own responsibilities and to escape the consequences of their actions. When parents unwisely loan them money that will be used for drugs or bail them out of jail over and over again, they teach addicted children that the parents condone their addiction. This is not the message parents are trying to convey, but addicts often take well-intended actions and distort them to their own way of thinking. Parents' enabling actions are the result of their love for their children and their desire to take seriously the responsibilities of being a good, caring parent. They thought they were only doing what God called them to do as Christian parents.

Enabling has to do with boundary issues. God expects parents to set clear boundaries for their children, in order for these children to learn to live independent lives. When parents enable their children, they refuse to yield control of their children's lives to God and others who might offer help. Parents yearn to fix things. Their inclination as parents always remains to protect their children. Enabling, however, keeps children further removed from seeking help with their addictions. Why should addicted children get help when parents provide a protective, comfortable, welcoming environment where all of their needs are met and where they can continue to live addictive lives without paying any price for their bad choices? Even if children make destructive decisions, they must learn to live with the consequences of their actions. This does not mean parents should never help their children or should give up on their children and abandon them to addiction. Just as God could not give up on His children, parents are not expected to reject their children, disown them, or sever relationships. God does want parents to stop enabling, however. Scripture tells us that God wants us to be free to know the truth. When parents recognize the truth of their enabling, they are set free to set recovery for the addict and for the family.

Enabling gives parents control over their addict's life. When parents quit enabling, they allow God to take control. This is ultimately a matter of trust. When parents turn their addict over to God, they are proclaiming that they trust in God and they confess that they do not have the strength to continue to be drawn into their children's addictive lifestyles. Their emotional, physical, psychological, and spiritual lives have suffered due to enabling. Enabling forces parents to try to stay one step ahead of addiction—an impossible task. Enabling puts parents on duty every waking moment, trying to appease their addicts. It wears parents down while jeopardizing their relationship with God. Parents must pray for the power to change and ask for the humility to give God control of their enabling habits. Parents should ask God to give them the strength to sit down with their addicted children and set clear, definable boundaries. Then, parents must pray for the courage to keep these boundaries and not give in to the temptation to take up enabling again.

Parents must remember that they are human. All humans make mistakes, and there will be times when parents repeat the familiar patterns of enabling. When this happens, they must admit their wrongs to God and then have the integrity to explain to their addicted children that their actions are not acceptable or helpful to their children's recovery—or their own. Parents can then begin to break the cycle of enabling. Breaking the pattern of enabling takes time, patience, and help from God.

When parents stop enabling, they are better able to work on their own relationship with God. Enabling consumes large amounts of time and effort, so parents may have found that their prayer life, their devotional life, and their daily walk with God have all diminished. Now parents must renew their relationship with God. Quitting our enabling becomes a matter of trust for us. Surrendering children to God does not mean that parents have no part in their children's lives. Yet, they begin to focus on God's ability to do what is impossible for parents. Parents usually lack the skills to fix their children's addictions. They are devoid of the power to heal their children and rid them of their addictive nature. Handing their children over to God becomes a faith issue. Parents affirm their confidence in the faithfulness of God to work in the lives of their children and in the lives of others who will impact their children's recovery. They commit their children to God, also knowing that God creates them with free will; therefore, they may reject His offer of forgiveness and continue down the spiraling path of addiction.

Giving children to God means that parents partner with God to help their children, but they also stop the cycle of enabling. They quit obsessing over their children to the point where they stop living their own lives. They make a positive change and decide to start taking care of themselves for a change.

Difficult Decisions

A time may come when parents must make the difficult decision to remove addicted children from their house or cut off communication with them due to safety and personal issues. That decision is between the parents and God, and parents should not be judged by others because of the decisions we make. Some people will meddle into their lives and accuse them falsely when they do not know the entire story. Others may want to control decisions and continually offer advice. If the advice of outsiders is not helpful, parents might suggest to them that they will get back in touch when they need further aid, but parents may have to establish firm boundaries when meddling becomes a problem. Parents are not required to explain their actions, but if they choose to do so, they must realize that some people may defend the addicts. Relatives may even intercede to supply addicts with food, shelter, and money when parents have refused the addicts.

Parents must stick by their decisions and try not to get involved once they have made the decision to stop enabling. Parents cannot control the actions of outsiders, only their own. Relationships may be severed with friends and relatives who accuse parents of abandoning their own children. This can upset and hurt parents, but this is a part of what sometimes happens when parents are bold enough to demand distance from their addicts. Parents should not let others keep them from reclaiming sanity in their own lives.

Parents must pray to God before making any challenging decisions and must seek advice from those they trust. When they are in the middle of an addiction crisis, parents often find it easy to react emotionally, without thinking through the outcomes of their actions. Parents must assure their children who begin a program of recovery that they will support them and seek to restore fragmented relationships if at all possible. Once parents make a decision to set boundaries, they need to stick by their decisions. Addicts easily manipulate parents into their way of thinking and can use the ploys of guilt and persuasion very effectively. They will also make promises to parents in order to prevent parents from setting limits. Parents should be aware that these promises are quickly broken when their children's allegiance to addiction overrides any ability for these children to remain true to their word.

Many parents may be thinking, *But I cannot abandon my children to addiction!* By following a faith-based approach, parents are not abandoning their children. They are placing them in God's hands and setting them free to make their own decisions as children of God. They are practicing the stewardship of parenting, which acknowledges that children come from God and belong to God. Parents are declaring their trust and faith in a God who gave their children to them as divine gifts, but parents understand that they do not own their children. They cannot possess their children, for those children are independent, free creations, all given the ability to make right or wrong decisions. Children belong to the God who created them in His image.

Let me be very realistic about addiction. When children made the choice to take that first drug, drink that first drink, or engage in any number of lifestyles recognized today as addictions, those were the children's own choices. Yet, when children became addicts, the disease of addiction—which is beyond their control—obliterated their free will. Now they may be so totally possessed by their addiction that they cannot stop without intervention. Some well-meaning friends will tell parents that if they their children really cared about them, they would simply stop the addiction. Addicts cannot just stop. Their brains have become wired toward addiction, making it impossible to walk away from a drink, throw out their pills, stop their spending sprees, or stop collecting pornography. As for alcoholics, it is extremely dangerous for them to stop "cold turkey." The results can lead to dangerous seizures that can be life-threatening.

I would urge parents to be very careful not to take the advice of people—even their church friends—who have no experience in addiction. Parents should remain involved in their children's lives if at all possible. Children need their parents' wisdom and discernment. These are God-given tools we employ to guide our children toward recovery. Children may resist us and resent us, but they need to hear their parents' continued urgings and constant pleas to reach out and seek help. They are usually open to our ongoing support, especially when they are in recovery.

God never intends parents to sacrifice to the point where they put their own well-being and health on hold for the sake of addictive children. Parents cannot help their children until those children help themselves. God creates us with free will to make decisions. Parents cannot force children into recovery. Parents actually hinder their children's recovery when they fail to get the help they need to become strong parents. One parent of an addicted child recently commented to me that he had become "toxic" for his son. He had never intended to do this, but he had enabled his son so much and so well that his son saw no reason to pursue recovery. Even when in recovery, this father tried to work his own son's program, thereby hindering his son's efforts to develop his own recovery journey. What this father realized was that his poisonous methods of enabling were keeping his son from getting well. It was also preventing the father from growing in his own faith and was destroying his relationship with God. This father made a concerted effort to turn his son over to God. He is still very involved in his son's life, but now he stands back and lets others who are far more qualified help his son. He gets out of the way so God and others can direct his son toward recovery. This father discovered that his son could not get well until *he* got well himself.

Those who have been on an airplane trip are familiar with the instructions of the flight attendants prior to takeoff. In case of the loss of altitude, adults on board are clearly directed to first put on their own oxygen masks and then assist children with their masks. This same principle works when dealing with children who are addicts. Parents must put on their own "oxygen masks" of recovery, breathe in the cleansing air of sanity, and then help their children put on their own masks of freedom from addiction.

Parents and Addicts in Recovery

My suggestion is that parents of addicts develop their own recovery plans, regardless of the actions of their addicted children. The parents' steps toward recovery should have little to do to with whether their child embraces recovery or not. A part of this recovery is to pray daily to God for strength, wisdom, and discernment. Then, parents must set personal goals for themselves. These include steps of commitment to seek and find ways to grow stronger spiritually, emotionally, mentally, and physically. If parents are married, they must also begin to work on strengthening their relationship with their spouse. Marital relationships are always strained when addiction enters a home. Parents should get counseling if needed and join appropriate support groups in their communities. Addiction, particularly the act of enabling, causes parents to put on hold those things they enjoyed in the past. I would strongly advocate that parents take up a hobby, volunteer, or begin again to do some of the activities that gave them pleasure prior to addiction entering their lives. Also, parents can read the Bible, pray, and engage in spiritual disciplines that allow them to grow in their faith in God.

When addicted children enter a recovery community, parents should offer support but let children work their own program of recovery. Parents who were used to controlling their children's addiction may find it easy to fall back into old habits and seek to take charge of their children's recovery efforts. Doing so will be destructive to their children and can contribute toward a relapse. Parents do best when they turn sons or daughters over to recovery communities and get out of the way as parents. This sounds harsh, but it is the only way children will sustain a program of recovery.

Addicted children sometimes obtain sponsors, people who are themselves addicts who will guide these children. I know it is a risky thought to have to place children, even adult children, into the hands of a complete stranger. These sponsors understand the nature of addiction, having lived it themselves. They can see through the intentions, thoughts, attitudes, and actions of the addicts, while non-addicted parents cannot. Parents' well-intended efforts to work their children's recovery programs for them destroy their self-confidence and enable them to relapse easily. For the sake of the addict's sobriety, parents should offer support when asked but let go of their temptation to "baby" children in their recovery programs. Parents must trust God to send sponsors to their children that are needed at a particular phase of the children's recovery efforts. Parents will learn that very few addicts stay with the same sponsor always; as they progress in their programs of recovery, they need different viewpoints and perspectives.

Parents must face the unwelcome truth that most addicts relapse, and many will do this several times. Some addicts require repeated treatment before they embrace recovery. We discovered this to be true with our own family member. He was in and out of several recovery centers. Many of his friends, who are now in recovery, have the same story to tell. Parents should not judge their children when they relapse; rather, they must keep encouraging their children to try again to take the necessary steps toward recovery. Many of these recovery centers have a spiritual dimension. Children will be directed to admit the nature of their disease of addiction that has rendered them powerless. They will be taught to apply principles that guide them to wholeness in their shattered lives. Competent persons, such as addiction counselors and AA sponsors. will discuss with them issues of denial, guilt, and self-esteem. As addicts turn their unmanageable lives over to God, parents must do the same. Parents must confess to God their part in enabling their addicts, and parents must let go so God can restore them to sanity.

Parents should not be too hard on themselves when they relapse into old habits and ways of thinking. Addiction catches us as parents off guard, and sometimes all of us forget lessons learned in the past. Recently I was talking with the addict in our family. He was telling me that he is now working with some addicts at a community center in his neighborhood. I complimented him for taking on this responsibility and wished him the best. Yet, I could not leave well enough alone! He commented that usually only a handful of addicts showed up for the meetings and sometimes no one was present. I quickly assured him that with his leadership, the meetings would undoubtedly grow.

He politely reprimanded me, startling me when he said that it may be best if this group never grew. I thought to myself, *What? That makes no sense!* He explained to me that he and his sponsor had discussed his involvement with this group and that it offered him a wonderful opportunity to give to others in service without expecting any rewards in return. He reminded me of the selfish attitude of the addict and how humility stretched his growth and aided his recovery. Even though I knew this truth, my addict again gave me a great understanding into the nature of addiction. I wanted the addict in my family to achieve, as I knew him to be a capable leader. However, what he needed was not glory for his efforts but humility for his recovery.

A few weeks later, I was again in conversation with him. He was complaining about all of his commitments that stretched his time and energy, leaving him few hours in the day for himself. I hastily sympathized with him and suggested that he seek balance in his life. I had forgotten that "balance" is a catch word in his recovery community for "relapse." The outside world places value on balance, but an addict will use balance as an excuse for forgetting about others and centering upon self. My addict talked with his sponsor and reported back to me that his sponsor had seen right though his complaints, realizing they were efforts to slack up on his program of recovery, and the sponsor chided him to get busy helping others.

I have learned over time to trust my addict's sponsor, because, along with God, only another addict can truly help him. Addicts have the ability to strip away the hidden layers of deception, fear, and selfishness in another addict's life and get right to the truth. This is not something family members can do, even when we believe we know our addicts inside and out. My addict tells me that other addicts can even look in his face and see through the mask under which he attempts to hide. His recovery friends will not let him get away with the façade of false happiness. Many times when he thought he was doing an excellent job of hiding his true feelings, my addict's friends looked into his face and asked him to come clean with his true feelings.

This may sound remarkable and somewhat unbelievable to parents of addicts, but this has happened to my addict numerous times. It is especially difficult for parents of addicts to remember to let go when it comes to their relationship with their children. It takes courage to step back and let them learn these lessons of recovery without parental interference. Parents must face the truth that their addict's recovery exists in an area in which they are not qualified to venture, so they must not intrude. What parents can do is offer support, love, and encouragement. They urge the addict to continue a program of recovery, congratulate him or her on any small achievements in sobriety. They can attend family programs when the addict in in a recovery center. We send our loved one a card of encouragement from time to time and at his invitation, we attend his AA meeting when visiting with him. We also honor his sobriety efforts by making the effort to be present at the meeting that celebrated his one year of sobriety and beyond.

In one of the conversations my husband had with our addict, our loved one mentioned that he had overcommitted his time to a certain project in his recovery community, and as a result was tired and worn-out. He thought perhaps it was time to let someone else step in and replace him. My husband quickly agreed with him, thinking he was offering support. Our addict hastily replied, "You do not have to co-sign for me." In the recovery community, this is an expression used to indicate that family members, who are acting out of love and concern for the addict, are actually harming the addict's recovery. By agreeing, my husband was doing exactly what the addict in our family wanted him to do. Our addict was gaining support from my husband to justify not having to accept his commitment. My husband gave him a valid excuse to shirk the promises he had made to others.

Parents can support their children and pray for their children, but ask God to give them the fortitude to stay out of the way of their children's recovery. I have frequently had to remind my addict that in my haste to affirm him and his program, I often forget some of the basic lessons he has learned in recovery. Parents of addicts are always learning and will often make mistakes in judgment.

Parents are not being cruel to their children or lessening in any way their love and care for their addicts when they allow them to trust others in a recovery community. Parents can easily get their feelings hurt when their children turn to others for advice, rather than to the parents themselves. After all, parents are the ones God has instilled with the responsibility to guide their children in what is right or wrong in their lives. They still need their parents' advice in many areas of their lives. However, they do not need their parents' advice when it comes to matters of addiction and recovery. As hard as it is to do, parents must swallow their pride, humble themselves, and trust others to take care of their children while in recovery. Their duties as parents never diminish, and they will always remain the parents of their children. No one can take that God-given role from parents. Yet, children's recoveries must be their first priorities, even above their relationships with parents.

I know this is not what parents want to hear, but this is what they must hear as parents of addicts. God will honor and bless parents when they are willing to submit to their children in their recovery. Getting help and staying clean is the hardest task these children have even undertaken. Parents must not undermine their efforts with their own feelings of jealousy or bitterness. They should ask God to remove all of their misgivings and take away their reluctant and selfish motives. This is not only my suggestion to parents of addicts but it is a biblical teaching intended to enrich their lives:

> *"Put away from you all bitterness and wrath and anger and wangling and slander, together with all malice, and be kind to one another, tender-hearted, forgiving one another, as God in Christ has forgiven you."*
>
> *Ephesians 4:31–32 (NRSV)*

Parents must realize that recovery is a lifetime process for everyone involved. Children will never reach a point in their lives when they are truly "cured." Parents and family members live with the reality that they too always engage in recovery efforts. As hard as this is to accept and fully comprehend, parents will always have children who are addicts. Some of them will be known as recovering addicts. Working a stringent program of recovery requires daily meetings that are necessary for many addicts to stay clean. Parents must not resent the new reality that they are given less time to spend with their children or the fact that the addicted child may choose to live in a recovery community some distance from where the family lives. Parents should be thankful each day that their children have chosen recovery and pray for them, their sponsors, and their other friends in recovery.

Siblings in the Family

If parents have other children in the family, these children may have been greatly affected by their sibling's addiction. Parents have often ignored these other children when attention has been showered upon the addicts. Thus, they must work especially hard to convey love to and seek forgiveness from these children who did nothing wrong but nevertheless seem to have ended up being treated unfairly. These children have sometimes expressed bitterness toward parents and their addicted siblings. Sometimes visiting their brothers or sisters, especially on a family weekend offered by most treatment centers, helps these siblings. Others may need professional treatment as well. All of these siblings require a spiritual program of recovery along with parents. There are resources and meetings in the community to help parents and siblings of addicted family members. Parents should allow their other children to attend these and talk with them regularly about the disease of addiction.

Siblings of addicts also deal with guilt and must be assured that they did absolutely nothing to cause their brothers or sisters to become addicts. Parents can suggest that siblings write letters to their brothers or sisters in recovery centers and pray for them each day. Parents can alleviate the fears of the siblings of addicts that they will themselves become addicts, but they can also educate siblings about the risks of a family history of addiction. Parents can refer them to the section of this chapter where I address the concerns of siblings of addicts.

Lessons from a Parable

Luke's gospel (Luke 15:11–31) recounts Jesus's captivating story of a wayward younger son who squandered his father's inheritance in a far country. After the son frivolously wastes all of his money, he finds work caring for pigs, an occupation that any Jewish boy would dread. In Jewish tradition, pigs were unclean animals, and Jewish law forbade the meat from pigs to be consumed. Just imagine how embarrassing it must have been for this Jewish boy to work in the pigpens. Then, the story tells us that the boy becomes so famished with hunger that he is humiliated into eating the pods that the pigs were consuming! Finally the son has a moment of awakening when "he came to himself" and decides to go home, beg for his father's mercy, and plea to be given a lowly job as one of the hired hands.

To the son's surprise, his father humbles himself, hikes up his robes, and runs out to meet his son. No doubt the father had been searching for his son all along for "while he was still far off, his father saw him and was filled with compassion …" The father throws a huge party, invites all of the neighborhood, lavishes the son with exuberant gifts and restores their broken relationship.

The addict in my family has often commented to us that this story presents to him a perfect picture of addiction mingled with God's and his own family's forgiveness and grace. Parents of addicts have helplessly stood by as their children entered the far country of addiction. Parents have watched children ruin their lives and trade in their potential when consumed by the wasteland of addiction. Day after day, parents—just like the parable's father did—constantly look for any signs of hope that their children will return to them. Pivotal moments in our addiction stories occur when the children come to themselves and begin the journey home.

In the tradition in which Jesus told this story, it would have been extremely undignified for a gentleman of this man's status to hike up his robes and run out to meet his son. Never should he have offered his son a kiss or displayed any sort of affection toward him. Villages in biblical times were small, and everyone knew one another. Gossip would have abounded among the villagers concerning the actions of the younger son. Coming home, after totally embarrassing his father, he would have given the community the right to kill him. His father, running to embrace his son, might reflect his need to protect him as well as offer him unrestrained grace. Yet the father is so relieved to have his child home that he kills a fatted calf. That is enough meat to feed the entire community, suggesting that the father must not have cared what others thought about his son. He was just so happy to have him home that he was willing to risk the irate neighbors and even invite them to the party.

In the same way, parents of addicts rejoice when their children come to their senses and begin their journey into recovery. They are willing to take great risks, even to the point of alienating some unforgiving friends and family members , to forgive their children and celebrate their journey toward wholeness. They may not throw a huge party and invite the entire neighborhood, but they may work very hard to restore relationships with the lost child. In this parable, the father gives the son his ring. The ring signified the father's authority, as it was pressed into wax for the father to sign important documents. The boy is given sandals to wear. This signified that the son would not be considered a hired hand but the father's son. Hired hands did not wear sandals; they performed their tasks with bare feet. In his decisive actions, the father works to restore his relationship with the son. He does all he can to let his son know that he is valuable to his father. Parents of addicts often take the same swift action when their children embrace recovery. They support them and restore them to a place of importance in the family circle.

The parable also spoke of an older son. This son was not happy to see his younger brother return home and failed to understand the mercy of the forgiving father. Can we blame him for his indignation at the actions of his father? This older son remained faithful to his father and respected and upheld the traditions of his community. In contrast, the small, close-knit village ostracized the younger son because he exhibited little respect for his father and engaged in an unrespectable, despicable lifestyle. Perhaps the siblings in families with addictions can readily relate to the plight of the older son in our story. Siblings of addicts proceed cautiously when asked to celebrate the recovery of their brother or sister. They have been fooled too many times, so they question whether their sibling is truly sincere. They have been cheated out of their parents' attention and neglected in their own life struggles. They have been relegated to second place or below in the family ranking system, because addiction in the family always stole center stage. No wonder they are not quite "in the party mood" when the addict in the family returns.

Siblings of addicts should not be immediately pressured to resume a close relationship with a brother or sister who has been in addiction. Time is required for trust to be restored. Encourage children to re-establish their relationship on their own terms and in their own time frame. Do not force other children in the family to align themselves with the acceptance of their addict on the parents' proposed timeline. Allow these children plenty of space to find their own time and means to welcome the addict back into the family.

Parables, like that of the Prodigal Son, are intended to teach us a lesson about God. If God is the father in the story, God welcomes the addict with open arms and with loving embraces. God offers each addict forgiveness, restoring him or her to a right relationship with God. God is always waiting and looking, like the father in our story, anticipating with joy when the prodigal sons or daughters will return home. Unlike this father, who could not leave his home and search for his missing son, God searches for our addicted children, pursuing them with His grace and sending the Holy Spirit to abide with them at all times and in all situations. God is always present with addicted children, wherever they go and whatever they do.

Will addicted children "come to themselves" and make the arduous journey toward home? Some children never accept recovery, and remain forever in the clutches of addiction. Others wake up and discover that a whole new world awaits them outside the binding circles of addiction. The journey of recovery is rarely smooth. There are ups and downs, steps forward and steps backward, and relapses where addicts have to start again. Parental love for our children, as great as it is, is not sufficient to sustain them on the path to recovery. Only God's unconditional love for a prodigal son or daughter is strong enough to rescue them from addiction and guide them on the journey toward home.

My prayer is that one day all prodigal sons and daughters will "come to themselves," leaving addiction behind for the comforts and security of home. In the meantime, like the father in the parable, parents must be waiting, watching, and looking down the road for their lost children. When they see their children coming toward them from that far country of addiction, will they, like Father God, ecstatically run out to meet them? No matter what happens to their children, they are still their sons and daughters, and the parents will always be these children's parents. Regardless of the outcome, will parents, like the prophet Hosea's Parent God, exclaim to their prodigal sons and daughters, "How can I give you up?" Their words are not uttered with the parents' submissive cry of defeat; rather their words are voiced with exclamations of faith. Any refusal by parents to give up on their sons and daughters is not based on naïveté on their part; rather, it flows from hope that is grounded in God's love and anchored in parental love that never ends.

Words of Assurance for Siblings of Addicts

If you are the sibling of an addict, no doubt, for many of you, your home environment has been turned upside down. Your parents were forced to center their attention on your brother or sister as time and again your own needs were ignored. Every waking moment was consumed with your sibling's problems. Holidays were ruined and family traditions were shattered when addiction entered your house. Money that should have been equally divided among siblings has been wasted to feed your brother or sister's addiction or poured out to treatment or detoxification centers. You have watched your gullible parents enable your manipulating sibling to the point they became sick themselves. Your intelligent parents have turned into obedient robots, catering to every whim of your addicted sibling. Some of you live with great resentment toward your parents and your sibling. Others of you have witnessed your sibling being carried away on a stretcher to the hospital, being handcuffed by the police and carted off to jail, or being defended in court by your family attorney. Most of you are afraid for your brother or sister's safety. You live in constant and uncertain fear of your sibling's impending death.

In the midst of your chaotic and insecure home life, your sibling's addiction has managed to wreak havoc on your spiritual relationship with God. Perhaps you blame God for bringing unmanageable difficulties to your family. Along with God, you heap blame upon yourself. You think that you are partially to blame as one of the sources of the problem. Maybe you overlooked ways to prevent this horrible disease from afflicting your family. Perhaps you even introduced your sibling to drugs, alcohol, pornography, or gambling. Maybe you enabled your sibling to obtain drugs or alcohol or covered up for your sister or brother. Perhaps you think if you had been a better-behaved child or a more agreeable sibling, this might not have happened to your brother or sister. Your guilt keeps you awake at night, and your pride prevents you from sharing your family secrets. When you pray, you end up begging and pleading with God to intervene for your sibling and family. You ponder in your heart if God hears your prayers, you sometimes doubt whether God will answer your prayers, or you question if God even cares about your family. Seeing what horrible things your sibling has done to destroy his or her life, you wonder if God is able to offer forgiveness. Knowing how effectively and totally your sibling tore down your family peace, you contemplate whether your family has any hope of survival.

God should not be blamed for causing your sibling to stray down the misguided path of addiction. God created us as free creatures, and out of love for us, limited His own power, so that we have the right to make decisions. These decisions are sometimes wise, but often they are foolish. God allowed your sibling to make his or her own choices. Addiction is a terrible disease, and once your brother or sister got caught in its vicious cycle, he or she could not escape, no matter how hard they tried. Most sibilings are also not in any way to blame for their sibling's addiction. There is nothing you did wrong and absolutely not a thing you could have done to prevent this devastating disease from inflicting itself upon your brother or sister. If, however, you did help your sibiling by giving him drugs or alcohol, you must now reach out for God's forgiveness. Where was God in all of this? God stays close beside your addicted sibling, and God remains by your side at all times. You must never doubt the presence of God and the abiding peace of the Holy Spirit. Cling to God and pray to Him every day for healing in your family.

You must remember that addiction is a family disease. Your sibling's addiction problems have spilled over into your own life and harmed you in many ways. You and your family must get help, even if your sibling never does. Finding resources in your community, especially for siblings of addicts, is crucial for your recovery. There are many support groups for siblings of addicts. Learn all you can about the disease of addiction and find a group that provides you the necessary support. Encourage your parents and other family members to get involved in a support group as well.

Many of you have been forced to grow up too fast and be educated firsthand about addiction from the experiences in your family. These are lessons that many of your peers never have to learn, and because of this, you may feel a sense of isolation and loneliness. For this reason, it is extremely important for you to seek to find support groups of your own peers who have faced some of the same situations you have encountered in dealing with your addicted sibling. In these groups, you can open up to others who understand your own journey, and you can find friends who can truly empathize with you.

You may be the one in your family who initially recognizes your sibling's addiction when your parents are unaware. You must be bold enough to speak out, even when your parents are in denial about the addiction. Do not keep what you know a secret from your parents, because the more time your sibling spends on the addiction path, the stronger the addiction grows, until your sibling is completely out of control. Your sibling may be angry with you for revealing his or her addiction, but for the welfare of your brother or sister, you must not keep this a secret.

It takes great courage to be the sibling of an addict. Your worries and fears about your sibling are justified, but you must release your sibling to the care of God so you can be set free to live your own life. Trusting your sibling to God's care does not mean you do not continue to love him or her. Doing so affirms the love you have for your brother or sister because you want him or her to get well. As strong as you are, you do not have the ability to make your sibling well. Even with the greatest fortitude, you cannot control your sibling's addiction.

When your sibling enters recovery, support him or her. Pray for your sibling. Keep the lines of communication open. One of the greatest fears your addicted brother or sister will carry into recovery is that they will lose the love and support of their family. Plan appropriate visits with them, and be willing to go with your parents to a family weekend if your sibling is in a treatment center that has such a program.

Remember that you are never alone in this journey of addiction. Addiction may have weakened your faith in God, but now is the time to work to restore that relationship. God never once abandons you in the midst your sibling's addiction. God is present with you and walks each day by your side. Draw from the available resources of God's grace, peace, and love. Only by doing so can you experience hope for better days ahead.

Recommended Resources for Parents of Addicts

Addicts in the Family, Beverly Conyers, Hazelden, 2003.

Don't Let Your Children Kill You: A Guide for Parents of Drug and Alcohol Addicted Children, Charles Rubin, New Century Publishers, 1996.

Helping Your Chemically Dependent Teenager Recover: A Guide for Parents and Other Concerned Adults, Peter R. Cohen, MD, Hazelden, 1978.

Inside a Cutter's Mind: Understanding and Helping Those Who Self-Injure, Jerusha Clark with Dr. Earl Henslin, Think, 2007.

Marijuana: What's a Parent to Believe?, Timmen L. Cermak, MD, Hazelden, 2003.

Parenting—Life Without Parole: Surviving Your Child's Addiction, Willy, AuthorHouse, 2004.

Setting Boundaries with Your Adult Children: Six Steps to Hope and Healing for Struggling Parents, Allison Bottke, Harvest House Publishing, 2008.

Sober Coaching Your Toxic Teen, Michael J. Marshall, PhD & Shelly Marshall, BS, CSAC, Day By Day, 2007.

The Enabler: When Helping Hurts the Ones You Love, Angelyn Miller, MA, Wheatmark, 2008.

Teens Under the Influence: The Truth About Kids, Alcohol & Other Drugs— How to Recognize the Problem & What to Do About It, Katherine Ketcham, Ballantine Books, 2003.

Recommended Resources for Siblings of Addicts

Drugs and Your Brother and Sister, Rhonda McFarland, Rosen Publishing Group, 1997.

My Big Sister Takes Drugs, Judith Vigna, Albert Whitman Co., 1995.

Sober Siblings: How to Keep Your Brother or Sister—and Not Lose Yourself, Patricia Olsen & Petro Levounis, Da Capo Press, 2008.

CHAPTER EIGHT:

The Double Demons of Addiction and Mental Illness

"They came to the other side of the lake, to the country of the Gerasenes. And when he had stepped out of the boat, immediately a man out of the tombs with an unclean spirit met him. He lived among the tombs; and no one could restrain him any more, even with a chain; for he had often been restrained with shackles and chains, but the chains he wrenched apart, and the shackles he broke in pieces; and no one had the strength to subdue him. Night and day among the tombs and on the mountains he was always howling and bruising himself with stones ... Then the people came to see what it was that had happened. They came to Jesus and saw the demoniac sitting there, clothed and in his right mind, the very man who had had the legion; and they were afraid."

(Mark 5:1–5, 15)

Those of us whose family members live with the double demons of addiction and mental illness can easily identify with this story of a young man powerfully bound by destructive enemies so far beyond his control that he constantly lived in a state of perpetual hopelessness. Whether demonic forces possessed this disturbed man or some form of mental illness contributed to his erratic behavior does not really matter. What does matter is that Jesus healed this man and restored his dignity. A naked, violent, thrashing individual was changed into a clothed, calm person "in his right mind." No longer did the young man need to live in the cemetery, alienated from his family and community; Jesus's healing allowed him to return to his village and his home. A broken, ostracized, demoniac returned to the community as a totally different person whom Jesus commissioned to tell his amazing story to all who would listen.

When a family member has a mental illness coupled with addiction, we readily observe how one illness feeds another, working together effectively to destroy any semblance of peace in the life of our addict. We see our loved ones lose control of their emotions, actions, and thought processes. They may lash out at us in anger and then turn around and cry tears of remorse. Some of our mentally ill addicts harm themselves physically or commit acts of violence against family members. We are afraid to leave them alone, for we are never certain what they will do, so we live in a constant state of upheaval. Often we wonder whether our loved one's out-of-control behaviors are the result of the addiction, mental illness, or both. Yet the actions of the young man in Mark's gospel sound familiar to those of us who live with a family member with both an addiction and a mental illness. Our loved ones exist shackled with diseases that possess their body, spirit, and mind, and chain them to fear and uncertainly about their future.

Besides the common thread of similar behavior between the young man in Mark's gospel and our loved ones, there is another part of the story to which we can relate. While we may not condemn our loved ones to live among the tombs, society and some of our friends ostracize our loved ones to the point where they may feel like they do. Perhaps friends, relatives, and even church members looked down upon the family and addict and criticized us for a disease beyond our control. Both mental illness and addiction are not given the support and understanding in our society today that many other diseases receive. Some people still see addiction as the fault of the addict and the family. The mentally ill are often frowned upon as nuisances to society, people we must keep hidden and out of the way so that we do not have to deal with them. Like the young man in Mark's gospel, our mentally ill addicts may remain in isolation from society and the community of faith due to the unfair judgment of others.

Unlike our man in Mark's gospel, however, our mentally ill family members are not cured. They live each day with mental illness along with addiction. Recovery efforts for the addiction and proper medication for the mental illness help our loved ones to regain sanity in their lives, but we know they live with these diseases throughout their lifetimes. With that knowledge in mind, how do we reconcile the story in Mark's gospel to our present situation?

It helps us to remember another story in Mark's gospel that occurs just prior to the story of the demoniac. In this story, recorded in Mark 4:35–41, the disciples are in a boat when a violent storm erupts. The disciples are terribly frightened until Jesus calms the wind and waves. No doubt, Mark wanted us to see this story of Jesus calming the storm in nature being tied with the story of Jesus calming the storm in the life of the demoniac. Jesus brings peace to both the chaos of the sea and the chaos of the mind. Jesus removes fear from both His disciples and the one He encounters in the graveyard. In the same way, Jesus comes to calm the storms of addiction and mental illness that plague our families.

One of the most interesting parts of this story of the demoniac is its ending. As Jesus is getting back into the boat to leave this region, the healed man begs Jesus to take him along. Imagine the expression on the faces of the disciples when they hear this request. Jesus has entered a Gentile region, so this man is not Jewish! The disciples carry their own prejudices toward this man because of his nationality. They cannot fathom Jesus inviting this man to join their band of disciples. Jesus knows that the disciples have not reached the point of maturity to be able to embrace someone outside of Judaism. This comes later, after His death and resurrection. Yet, Jesus ventures with them into uncomfortable places and into the presence of unwelcomed people to teach them about God's grace. Jesus calms the storm in the life of this man in the same way He has calmed the storm on the sea for his disciples. All of us are worthy of God's love, including our family members, as we deal with the problems of addiction and mental illness. Jesus works to calm the storms in our lives.

Jesus does not leave the young man sitting alone in the cemetery. He tells him to go into the community and share the good news of his healing. In the same way, Jesus does not desire our loved ones who suffer with addiction and mental illness to be isolated from family, friends, society, or our communities of faith. Families, addicts, and the mentally ill do not need to live in secrecy, ashamed of their identity or embarrassed about what happens in their families. Families may have to be the ones to speak out for our mentally ill addicts and advocate for their rights to be heard and seen in society and in the church. As our mentally ill addicts embrace recovery and have the proper medicine and professional help, they can speak out as well as share their stories in places they are comfortable in sharing. Most of the time, this will be their recovery community, where others can understand and offer them support. At other times, they may share with family members, friends, and their faith community. That is up to them, but Jesus offers families and the mentally ill addicts the right to live with dignity and respect.

The dual diagnosis inflicted upon our loved ones creates an emotional burden on our families. We worry that our mentally ill addicts might attempt or even commit suicide. We are aware that statistics tell us the grim fact that individuals with dual disorders are at a greater risk for suicidal tendencies. We also fear our family members might get into trouble with the law because they often make unwise, hastily thought-out decisions that place them in harm's way. We may distrust our family members to handle money responsibly, especially if we are dealing with a bipolar disorder where our addicts become manic and go off on a spending spree or gamble away hard-earned money on lottery tickets. We are angry about the physical and verbal abuse we endure at the hands of our mentally ill addicts. Some of us are constantly on edge, never relaxing, because we never know whether our addicts will be depressed or manic. Others of us are worn down by the panic attacks our addicts experience when they find themselves in new situations. Depression drives some of our addicts to ignore their own children, spouses, or other family members.

Taking seriously what Jesus offers us means that we first have to deal with the faith issues that arise when addiction and mental illness enter our homes. Uninvited, they filled our houses with guilt, shame, and fear. We cringe from our lack of control over these diseases. These issues of faith are common to all families of addicts, but they are especially challenging when coupled with mental illness. Now we are dealing not only with problems of addiction, but we have to face the disease of mental illness as well. This does not seem fair to us. Many times we ask ourselves, "Why would God be so cruel to give our family member a mental illness along with addiction?" We believe this is too much for us to bear and wonder if God is testing us beyond our limits.

We must begin by asserting that God is not the cause of addiction and God is not the cause of mental illness. Neither are our families and our addicts responsible for these devastating illnesses. Addiction and mental illness are both diseases without cures, although help is available. Blaming God for inflicting our loved one with both diseases is not fair to the God who creates humankind and creation in His own image. Our addict's journeys of addiction begin with the first choices. Some of these choices are to abuse their bodies with drugs, alcohol, deprive their bodies of food, overindulge by eating excessive amounts of food, unwisely spending money, or squandering their lives with gambling or pornography. Once the habits are formed, our loved ones are unable to turn back. They become addicts rather than casual users. Mental illness is a result of a malady in the brain not due to sin or the wrath of God. We do not serve a God who gives us these diseases, but we worship a God who is faithful as we struggle to deal with addictions and mental illnesses. Our loved ones are not given the diagnosis of dual disorders because God is testing them. Rather, in the hard times of our great trials, God is present with our addicts and our families.

One of the greatest challenges for all families of addicts is enabling. This is especially true with the families of mentally ill addicts. It is easy to excuse and justify our enabling because of the mental illnesses of our addicts. People with mental illnesses often need extra help dealing with life situations. Families step in and want to do all they can to make life easier for the family members who already face many challenges. Sometimes it is hard to differentiate between enabling our addicts and assisting our mentally ill family members. We offer needed help to our mentally ill addict when we seek competent medical care and encourage him or her to take needed medication. We enable him or her when we rationalize that the addict must continue his or her addiction in order to live with a mental illness. We need to be extremely careful and sensitive when dealing with mentally ill addicts. Many people offer us advice that may be wise when dealing with most addicts, but their words may not contain good wisdom for dealing with addicts with mental illnesses. We must pray to God to give us discernment to tell the difference between enabling and assisting.

Friends might advise us to throw our addicts out of the house and let them fend for themselves. However, if we deal with mentally ill addicts, we must think carefully before following this advice. We know that our mentally ill addicts need medicines that they may forget to take if we do not watch them closely. Not taking their medications can lead to all sorts of bad scenarios that can be far worse than what can happen if the addicts remain in our homes. It is easy for people to prey on the mentally ill. Law-enforcement officials often receive training on how to approach individuals who are mentally ill. Still, mentally ill addicts can get themselves in trouble with the law because they put themselves at risk to do whatever it takes to feed their addictions. Mental illness adds a different dimension to the addiction picture. Families of the addicted and mentally ill must not let anyone talk us into doing something we feel in our hearts is wrong. Families of the addicted and of the mentally ill should continually ask God for guidance, and we must enter into sincere prayer for God to send the Holy Spirit to direct us.

Coping with the pervasive feelings of guilt and shame that accompany mental illness and addictions is difficult for both family members and addicts. We must turn our guilt and shame over to God and release ourselves from the burdens. We will have enough to deal with from the addiction and mental illness. We do not need the additional weights of guilt and blame. Our addicts are not failures because they have mental illnesses or addictions. We blame ourselves sometimes because we see that the potential God has given our addicts is being wasted by addictions and is being silenced by their mental illnesses. We think that perhaps we can do something to prevent these diseases, but the truth is, there is absolutely nothing we can do that is effective. It takes time to release our guilt and shame and give them over to God. We must take small steps each day. We must accept the liberating truth that our addicts have "no-fault" illnesses. We must never label them as weak or unacceptable, and we must not tolerate others who label them as such. They are children of God. They need our validation as people of worth who happen to have mental illnesses, but we also need to challenge them to get help for their addictions.

Dealing with addicts who also have mood disorders often makes family members impatient. We confess that most of us have not been as loving and caring toward our mentally ill addicts as we know we should have been. This causes us to live with guilt as we look back and recall times when we criticized our addicts or pushed them to attempt feats for which they were not ready. Addicts who also have social disorders are uncomfortable in many social settings, especially when they are among strangers. Perhaps we pushed our socially anxious addict into the company of others when they were simply not prepared, and we found our addict experiencing panic attacks. We live with our guilt from remembering those unpleasant incidents. Maybe we give our bipolar addicts money to help pay bills, but find they use our hard-earned money to buy unneeded luxuries. Now we share in the guilt as family members who enable our addicts to engage in irresponsible spending.

I recall the time when our addict was diagnosed with bipolar disorder. He was placed on medicine to subdue some of his manic tendencies. When his bipolar disorder was full-blown, he displayed manic behavior by spending large amounts of money, not sleeping for several days, and experiencing panic attacks in public places. He might go for several weeks before his disorder began to show obvious effects upon him. What was interesting is that he could begin to tell his family when he was about to experience rapid cycling wherein he went from a manic state to a mixed state of mania and depression, and then a heavy blanket of depression.

These times were difficult for our family. His restlessness, fear, and inability to sleep caused family members to have to stay up with him at night. This made it difficult for family members to assume their own work schedules. When this continued for several nights, we were totally exhausted. I was especially impatient with him when he told me he was about to go into a manic period. I blamed him and chastised him as if he could stop the mania over which he had no control whatsoever. Of course, in the back of my mind, I knew he was not to blame in any way, but I dreaded the days ahead because I knew what our family faced. I had to deal with the guilt for blaming our family member for something over which he had no power.

It is easy for families to condemn themselves because of guilt for their mistakes in dealing with their mentally ill addicts. We must learn to forgive ourselves when we lose our patience or fail to understand how difficult a journey this is for them. We are human beings and not God. We are afraid at times, and our fear causes us to react in unloving ways. We might panic when we are uncertain what to do. We are tired, and our weariness causes us to say and do things we would not say and do under normal circumstances. We have to let go of the guilt. We realize that we are doing the best we can. I can now let go of the guilt, as I recognize that our family did not desert our addict in his time of need. We stayed with him as he was suffering through his bipolar episodes and did not let him suffer alone. Many a night, my husband and I sat into the wee hours with our loved one as he listened to soothing music or talked with us. Sometimes we drove him around as getting out of the house seemed to sooth his times of anxiety and stress. Even though I look back with regret for my unkind words, I give the guilt to God each day so that God can forgive me and assure me of His love for me.

Families of mentally ill addicts store up guilt because we feel hopeless to battle against the forces of addiction and mental illness. We wish we could do more to help our addicts. We are not super-humans, and we do get weary. When we realize this, we are better able to ask God to forgive us for our shortcomings, yet recognize that we are doing our best in extremely difficult situations. Guilt keeps us from moving forward in our walk with God. Releasing our guilt to God does not alleviate the addictions or the mental illnesses of our family members, but it does free us to go on with our lives under God's care and strength and not our own.

Many of us pride ourselves on our ability to shoulder all of our problems alone. We keep busy caring for our addicts day in and day out until we think we have no more to give to them or to others. God wants us to turn our burdens and struggles over to Him and believe that we do not have to carry all our burdens alone. God wants to partner with us in this difficult journey. He is not a God who abandons us and expects us to be superheroes. As people of faith, we rely on God to help us. We depend on Him to give us strength for each new day. We pray to God to help us find the resources we need to help our mentally ill addicts. We admit that we need help from God and from others.

I advise families of mentally ill addicts to turn to friends in their communities of faith to offer support and to pray for them. We cannot do this alone, for our tasks are too overwhelming. We open up to our close friends because we can trust them to understand and not judge us. There are also many resources in our communities to help us. The National Association for the Mentally Ill (NAMI) is one of the organizations that can provide us with tools and materials to cope with mental illnesses. We can also turn in our communities to dual-disorder support groups, comprised of individuals who, like us, have family members who deal with mental illnesses and addictions.

Many families coping with dual disorders make the decision to place their addicts in psychiatric hospitals for periods of time, to help them adjust when things get out of control. This decision is never easy to make, but is necessary when the addicts in our families are violent, suicidal, or need hospital care. At this time, we seek God's help and close presence. As people of faith, we believe that God draws close to our family during these difficult times and surrounds our loved ones with His abiding presence. We turn to our faith community and ask trusted friends to be in prayer for us. We cherish the visits of our church friends and pastors as they communicate to us their support and do not judge our addicts.

Children of addicts are especially frightened at times when the family member must be institutionalized or seek hospital care. We help children when we let them visit parents in the hospital, explain to them about what is happening in vocabulary words they understand, and assure them of our family's love. Children can read books on addiction and mental illness that will also help them to understand the double diseases of their parents.

One of the difficult challenges we face as families of addicts who also have a mood disorder occurs when our addicts are not taking their medicines. They tell us that they do not need the medicines and refuse to take them. Sometimes friends or acquaintances seek to convince them they do not need to be on any medications, and they pressure our addicts to give in to their demands. Well-meaning Christian friends can also persuade our addicts that they do not need their medicines. "If they trust God, they do not need to take any prescriptions," these people say. "They only need God." This is dangerous information for addicts or anyone with a mental illness.

This is a time when we have to ask God to help us find the right words to share with our addicts about what will happen if they do not take their medicines. We can start by telling them that there is no shame in taking medications. God does not look down on us. Remind them of the many ways God uses doctors, psychiatrists, and psychologists to help them. Share with them about how God helped individuals discover medicines that were not available many years ago. While mentally ill people had to suffer without help in the past, God has now led individuals to make wonderful discoveries of medicine that can offer relief. If such addicts are in recovery, they can talk with other mentally ill addicts or their sponsors, who can help them with questions they have about medications.

At the same time, we must be cautious concerning medication. Medicine and professional therapy are good and helpful, but some of our addicts use them so passionately that these remedies become their gods. Even their diagnosis can serve as a god they worship, rather than our true God. Our loved one related to us that he depended so strongly on his medications that he often forgot to pray to God. His medication became a crutch that replaced his reliance on God for strength and grace. Our loved one also, at times, blamed his mental illness for his addiction to alcohol. Some addicts use their mood disorder as an excuse for not moving forward in recovery. They do not get better because they substitute their mood disorders for God. Their diagnosis of bipolar disorder, depression, schizophrenia, or panic disorders keeps them from putting God first in their lives. They use these diseases as means of not getting better, not making amends to others, or not serving others in their recovery communities. They also use them as reasons why they cannot recover. It is too hard for them if they have a mental illness, they tell us. Their diseases become substitutes for their recovery programs. We help our addicts when we do not let them use their mental illnesses as a scapegoat for not working a diligent program of recovery.

When we are aware of this, we can help our addicts stop using their mood disorders as reasons for being unable to recover from their addictions. We encourage them to turn their lives over to God. God must come first if our addicts are to achieve sobriety. Mood disorders are not the first priority in a recovery program, and are not to be used as excuses for not working the program. Families of addicts must be very careful not to buy into their addicts' way of thinking. It is easy to excuse our addicts from working their program of recovery because they are afflicted with mental illnesses. Do not think this way, or addicts will be doomed to failure. We must keep God first in our lives, just like our addicts, because we also are tempted to put our addicts' mental illnesses before our God and our spiritual recovery. Our addicts' problems consume our lives if we are not careful. Keep God first. This is the only way we can help our addicts and ourselves to find wholeness and peace.

As important as medicine and professional help are, we must not use them as crutches to keep our addicts from working a program of recovery that puts God first. This does not necessitate us telling our addicts to stop taking their medicines or refrain from seeking professional help. We must be diligent and careful, however, to guide our addicts toward recovery programs that are spiritual in nature. We cling to the truth that without God's help, recovery is not possible. We remain firm and steadfast in our belief that God holds center stage. We give God priority in our lives. God takes first place, not our addicts' mental illnesses.

God guides us in the circumstances we cannot control. What is it about mental illness coupled with addictions that we cannot control? We certainly cannot control whether our loved ones are addicts or have mental illnesses. We cannot always control the way the disease affects our loved ones and causes them to act in ways that we find unhealthy, destructive, and harmful. Medication is effective up to a point, but we witness our addicts withdraw from us at times when manifestations of their diseases are especially visible. We cannot alleviate all of the hurts, anxieties, and fears our addicts carry with them each day. There is no way to control all of the factors of addiction and mental illness, although we often try very hard to be in charge of matters. We cannot control what our addicts choose to do with their lives. They make their own choices, and sometimes their decisions are difficult for us to live with. We cannot force our addicts to enter recovery or get help, although we can encourage them to move toward that direction. We cannot control the future of our addicts.

When we trust in God, we let go so God works in our lives in amazing ways. It helps us to focus on what we can control, rather than what we cannot control. We can control the way we get help for ourselves. We can attend support groups that deal with mental illness and addiction. We can read literature that helps us better understand what our mentally ill addicts are going through. We can support our addicts when they enter treatment centers, and we can continue to encourage them along the path toward recovery. We can focus our eyes on God and look to Him for our help. We cannot trust addiction and mental illness, but we can rely on God. It does not help us to worry about the things we cannot control. We turn our worries over to God, for we know that only God can understand our anxieties. He cares about each of us. Only God is able to alleviate our worries and give us peace.

If our addicts decide to enter a treatment center, it is essential that they attend ones that are able to handle the diseases of addiction and mental illness. Our selection must be made with utmost care. Only-dual diagnosis centers treat both maladies. Many centers are excellent at working with addicts, but often they have little or no background in mental illnesses. We must pay attention to the way the centers we research promote themselves. The addict in my family attended a "dual-diagnosis" center that we thought could help him with his addiction and his diagnosis of bipolar disorder. However, we later learned that what this center meant by "dual diagnosis" was the treatment of two or more addictions, such as alcohol along with an eating disorder. Therefore, families must ask careful questions and not be afraid to probe into the qualifications of each treatment center before a family member enters. My family learned this lesson the hard way and eventually got my addict into a center that was truly a dual-diagnosis facility.

Within the realm of addiction and mental illness lies a difficult concept to comprehend. Addictions and mental illnesses are so closely tied together that it is often hard to delineate between the two. After our addicts have been in recovery and clean for about a year, it is time for them to be re-tested for their diagnosis of mental illnesses. This may sound strange to some families because their loved ones may have a mental illness that manifests itself without any addiction being present. For some families, though, the mental illnesses begin alongside the addictions, especially in the teenage years. Some addictions create symptoms of mental illness, such as panic attacks, manic episodes, depression, mental blocks, and aggressive behavior. When the addicts allow their bodies to become clean from drugs or alcohol, they sometimes find these problems alleviate themselves as the brain is rewired for a new way of thinking and the body begins to heal itself. Some addicts find they do not need to depend on many of the medicines they currently take, once they are clean for a year or more. This is one of the miracles of the way in which God creates our bodies and minds. For some, the body and mind can heal themselves over time, given proper care and spiritual nourishment. If this is the case with our addicts, we need to stop and give God thanks for creating our bodies in such a marvelous way.

The addict in my family is almost free of any medication. We thought that he had damaged his body and mind such that it would never heal. To our delight, he returned to complete his college studies and is now in good health. We give praise to God along with all of the medical teams that God endowed with the knowledge and skills to help him.

This may not be the case in all families of mentally ill addicts. Some families have addicts who need medications all their lives. Many never recover from the damage to their bodies and minds. Others are unable to function on their own and need to be hospitalized or even institutionalized. While thanking God for our loved ones who recover and re-enter society as productive citizens, we also pray for families who live with addicts who are unable to function without medication or outside help. We pray for God's strength and presence to overshadow these families. We pray for peace and grace to manifest itself each day for these families and their addicts. We pray for courage for them to face the trials of living daily with mentally ill addicts. We pray for those families whose addicts say no to recovery and are on a downward spiral.

Those families whose addicts now see the light of day understand what it is like to be on the other side. We empathize with the families whose addicts still struggle with the enormity of mental illnesses and addictions. Our prayers are not just words of thanksgiving for our own addicts, but they are also prayers for others who still suffer greatly.

Our society is much further along than it once was when it comes to understanding both addictions and mental illnesses. We make great strides when we do not judge the mentally ill or the addicted, but know their problems stem from illnesses they do not cause and do not control without help from others. However, we still have a long way to go to educate society and advocate for the rights of the mentally ill. Families in particular can be the catalyst to help their faith communities. They can teach others about the diseases as they open up and share about their family experiences. Workshops held at churches are very helpful and serve as eye-openers for many people who have no prior knowledge of addiction or mental illness. Families can contact their elected officials and ask them to promote more adequate funding for treatment for addictions and mental illnesses.

Some individuals in our society, including in our churches, blame addicts for their diseases and think they can simply stop if they desire to do so. We educate others when we tell them this is not the truth and help them understand the nature of addiction. Many people still look down on the mentally ill, and again we are the ones who have to speak out, because we are the ones who have the stories to tell and the experiences to share. We can change the opinions of others, but it takes time and effort from all of us. We ask God to give us courage to make changes wherever and whenever we can, so that the future will be better for our mentally ill addicts.

We achieve no good purpose as families of addicts with mental illnesses if we fill our days wondering why our families are afflicted with two powerful and ravaging diseases. Life is a mystery in so many ways, and this is very true when we deal with addictions and mental illnesses. As God gives us strength, we are to go forward with courage and resolve to make the best of very difficult circumstances. We do not blame God, and we do not blame ourselves. Some things in life are simply not fair. Even when we reach the breaking point and can go no further, we remember that God is with us always. God never leaves us to face our problems alone.

Just as Jesus calms a storm on the sea and calms a storm of the mind, Jesus calms the storms in our own families. These are huge, raging storms, are they not? We could easily drown in them if we are not careful. And so we honestly admit that we are afraid. Only a Master of winds, waves, and lost minds is able to calm the storms in our turbulent lives. His calming presence and power is available to all of us whose lives are tossed and twisted by addictions and mental illnesses.

> *"He woke up and rebuked the wind, and said to the sea, 'Peace! Be still!' Then the wind ceased and there was a dead calm."*
>
> *Mark 4:39 (NRSV)*

The same one who rebukes the howling wind of the sea comes to quiet the ferocious winds of addictions and mental illnesses. The Christ who orders the chaotic waters now commands each of us, "Peace, be still!" Like the winds and waves, are we also obedient? Will we accept the calming presence of the Master of wind and waves who wants to enter our storm-tossed lives and give us His abiding peace?

Dealing with Suicide

As families of mentally ill addicts, we live in fear that our loved one will commit suicide. If this happens or has happened in our families, we immediately question God, our role in the suicide, our faith, and if our addicts are condemned to some form of eternal punishment. Depending on our faith communities, we hear many answers to our questions.

Our God is not responsible for our addicts taking their lives. God lets individuals make choices, and these choices can lead to deaths. Most addicts with mental illnesses deal with depression that leaves them with feelings of hopelessness. Addicts describe their depression as a black hole from which they can see no escape. Even if we talk with our addicts and they assure us they will not resort to extreme means such as suicide, this is not a guarantee they will not attempt it. We do not achieve anything good by blaming ourselves or second-guessing what we did or did not do. Families spend a great deal of time wondering if suicide could have been prevented if they had been present with their addict. They fault themselves for not saying the right words or doing the right things that would prevent the suicide. Our loved ones who deal with depression in addiction tell us that there is nothing anyone could say or do. At the time, the depression is so great and the pain so unbearable that people see no way to find relief except to resort to suicide.

Our God loves all people and creation. We are children of God, created in God's image. Our addicts who commit suicide remain as children of God, and God's circle of grace is wide enough to embrace our addicts at the time of their deaths. God is not one who limits grace. God knows exactly what our addicts have gone through to reach the point in their lives where suicide seems their only option. God relates to their pain and their struggles. God understands even when we fail to comprehend how our addicts could take their lives and leave their families behind to mourn.

Be assured that our addicts now rest in God's grace. So too must we. God is taking care of our addicts; He will also take care of our family.

God is not judging our addicts, so we must not judge. Do not accept the judgment of others upon our addicts or listen to those who tell us our addicts are condemned to hell. These people are wrong. They do not have a theology that understands the all-encompassing grace of God. They forget about God's mercy and only talk about God's judgment. They cannot begin to understand our situation or the pain our addicts suffered, so we should not believe these unhelpful words, even if this person reciting them happens to be a pastor.

What we can do is reach out and grab the understanding and kind support of people in our faith community and turn to qualified and caring support groups. Many churches have grief groups, and some of these are specifically designed around the issues of suicide. Do not be afraid or embarrassed to seek professional or pastoral counseling if needed, but be sure the pastoral counselor is the kind of person who does not blame or condemn us or our addicts. We must find ways to heal, so draw upon and make use of all available resources.

Find a new normal

Our healing does not entail "getting over" the suicide of our loved one. We discover that it is impossible to get over such a devastating loss, and we live with the pain the rest of our lives. We seek healing to honor the memory of our cherished loved one, our never-forgotten family member who would not want us to live each day centering on the suicide or blaming ourselves. We search after grace—not to find closure but to bring some peace to our burdened lives. In addition, our family can contribute to helping others who deal with their own losses brought about by a family member's suicide, but we need to be strong ourselves in order to help others.

We serve a God who is able to take our greatest pain and turn that sorrow into redemption. We have to turn our lives and hearts over to God, though, before any healing is possible. God abides with us each day, crying tears with us and grieving with us in our great loss. God is not expecting us just to forget our addicts, but to remember them by taking daily steps to renew our faith in Him. God walks with us through this turbulent storm, just as He walks with our addicts in fellowship with Him. We must accept God's love, grace, mercy, and peace for our family and for our addicts. God's arms are wide enough to embrace both us and our addicts. God provides us with a love that never lets go.

Recommended Books for Families with Mentally Ill Addicts

Addiction and Mood Disorders: A Guide for Clients and Families, Dennis C. Daley, Oxford University Press, 2006.

A Mind Apart: Poems of Melancholy, Madness & Addiction, Mark K. Bauer, Oxford University Press, 2008.

An Unquiet Mind: A Memoir of Moods and Madness, Kay Redfield Jamison, Vintage Books, 1995.

At Wit's End: What You Need to Know When a Loved One Is Diagnosed with Addiction & Mental Illness, Jeff Jay & Jerry Boriskin, Hazelden, 2007.

Bipolar Disorder Demystified: Mastering the Tightrope of Manic Depression, Lana R. Castle, Marlowe & Co, 2003.

Bipolar Disorder for Dummies, Candida Fink & Joc Kraynak, For Dummies, 2005.

East of Paradise & West of Ego, Mark Walliser, PublishAmerica, 2007.

Impulse Control Disorders, Jon E. Grant, W. W. Norton & Co., 2008.

Mood Swing: Understand Your Emotional Highs and Lows, Paul Meier, Stephen Arterburn & Frank Minirth, Thomas Nelson, 2001.

Overcoming Addiction: Skills Training for People with Schizophrenia, Lisa J. Robert, Andres Shaner & Thad Ecklman, W. W. Norton & Co., 1999.

Recovering from Sexual Abuse, Addictions & Compulsive Disorder: Numb Survivors, Sandra L. Knauer, Routledge, 2002.

Rollercoaster: Finding & Treating Bipolar and Other Unstable Mood Disorder, H. Paul, Putnam MD, Lulu.com, 2008.

Soft Bipolar: Vivid Thoughts, Mood Shifts and Swings, Depression and Anxiety of the Mild Mood Disorders Affecting Millions of Americans, Charles K. Bunch PhD, iUniverse, Inc., 2005.

The Courage to Lead: Start Your Own Support Group—Mental Illness & Addictions, Hannah Carlson, Bick Publishing House, 2001.

Understanding Schizophrenia & Addiction (Co-occuring Disorder Series), Dennis C. Daley & Kenneth A. Montrose, Hazelden, 2003.

When Someone You Love Has a Mental Illness: A Handbook for Family, Friends, and Caregivers, Rebecca Woolis, Penguin, 2003.

Web Sites

Borderline Personality: *http://www.healthyplace.com/*

Depression and Related Affective Disorder Association: *www.drada.org*

Dual Recovery Anonymous (DRA): *www.dualrecovery.org*

International Foundation for Research and Education on Depression: *www.ifred.org*

Mental Health Infosource: *www.mhsource.com*

National Alliance for the Mentally Ill: *www.nami.org*

National Depressive and Manic-Depressive Association: *www.ndmda.org*

National Institute of Mental Health: *www.nimh.nih.gov*

National Mental Health Association: *www.nmha.org*

Substance Abuse and Mental Health Services: *www.samhsa.gov*

Suicide Prevention Action Network: *www.spanusa.org*

CHAPTER NINE:

Can I Let Go and Let God?

Issues that Arise When Addicts Are in Recovery

> *"When the unclean spirit has gone out of a person,*
> *it wanders through waterless regions looking for a*
> *resting-place, but it finds none. Then it says, 'I will*
> *return to my house from which I came.' When it*
> *comes, it finds it empty, swept, and put in order.*
> *Then it goes and brings along seven other spirits more*
> *evil than itself, and they enter and live there; and the*
> *last state of that person is worse than the first ..."*
>
> *Matthew 12:43–45 (NRSV)*

On the surface and taken at face value, this passage of Scripture does not appear to have any connection to addiction. However, if we probe deeper into the text, we will find several truths that might help us as we consider the arena of recovery. The diabolical characteristics of addiction qualify the disease to be classified as an unclean spirit, a force that consumes our addicts with a vengeance, never desiring to let go of its harmful grip. When our addicts made the decisions to embrace recovery, they began the lifelong journey of keeping their "houses" clean.

Yet, we know that many addicts relapse at some point in their recovery journeys, and some relapse more than once. When this happens, the unclean spirit of addiction returns to our addicts' "houses," and they find themselves worse off than before with "seven other spirits more evil." When addicts resume their addictive patterns, the diseases return at the same level or a more destructive level. For example, recovering alcoholics discover that when they start drinking again, the drinking does not return at a slow, steady pace and then pick up gradually until they reach the point where they are unable to control their drinking. The alcoholism often returns aggressively, and they find themselves in the same or worse state than they were in before they stopped drinking.

However, this Scripture can also be interpreted for those addicts who are now clean from the physical effects of their diseases but are not working a sincere and diligent program of recovery. The addict in my family attempted to rid himself of the disease of alcoholism several times, but tried to do so without buying into the concept of a recovery program that required him to attend meetings every day, enter into a relationship with God, and give himself in service to others. He functioned as a "dry drunk." Therefore, he relapsed every time when he refused to work a stringent, disciplined program of recovery. He has been able to maintain sobriety only as he worked with a dedicated sponsor who required him to become accountable for his actions and guided him to the spiritual aspects of recovery.

Let us carry this story of Jesus one step further. We must consider not only the "houses" of our addicts, but also our own "houses" as family members of addicts. Since addiction becomes a family disease, we have been affected as well. All family members must work their own programs of recovery and healing in order to keep away the evil spirits of addiction. We might think that our lives are "empty, swept, and in order" when we send our addicts into treatment; that is when they are not physically present with us. We convince ourselves that our lives are getting better now that our addicts are working their programs of recovery. In reality, we are far from the truth. We are tied closer to the addiction than we realized, and the consequences have left us spiritually, physically, and emotionally depleted.

In some cases, we even sought the role of caretaker or rescuer and found ourselves lacking purpose when these functions were removed from our lives without our dependent addicts for us to enable. The is not to suggest that the caretake role always leads to enabling, rather to point out that this has happens to some families of addicts. Now we can replace our previous roles with that of recovering family member. Working our own programs of recovery also helps us to grow closer to God and renews our relationship with Him.

There are two aspects to the recovery process for families, and they are closely linked. Both aspects challenge families of addicts with their own issues of faith. One of the aspects has to do with the recovery efforts of the addict in our family. Families have certain roles to play as our addicts work on their recovery programs. We are confronted with the faith issues of trusting in God and letting go of control of our addicts' lives. We have to learn how to balance the times of trust with the times of support. We have to understand when it is best to hand over our addicts to God, when to let others help them, and when to reach out to our addicts with our helping hands.

The other aspect deals with our commitment to seek recovery for ourselves. To come to the point of accepting recovery for ourselves leads us into the paths of humility. In the past, I was reluctant to admit that I needed that recovery for myself. I reasoned, incorrectly, that I had not been the person with addiction problems in the family, so why did I need help? It took about six months into our loved ones recovery before I recognized that I was as sick as my addicted family member. I had been drawn into the vicious cycle of addiction, especially through my enabling efforts, but initially I was too proud to admit the truth. When I finally did, this freed me to begin my own program of recovery for myself. I had to develop a program of recovery that worked for me, and the same holds true for each family member facing addiction.

Nobody can work another family member's programs of recovery. We must commit to working these programs vigorously in ways that benefit us as individuals who have different situations and various needs. Each program of recovery should be personalized to meet the individual's needs. Our programs of recovery may look different from one another, but we have some similar tools that can help us along our recovery paths. God provides many of these tools. When we take these tools and use them effectively, they anchor us to a spiritual program of recovery. They are our available resources for daily use, and they continually offer us guidelines to keep us on the right paths of recovery.

Just as each family member must create a program of recovery that is tailored to meet his or her individual needs, our addicts need their own specific programs of recovery. Nobody can work our addicts' programs of recovery. They must work these programs for themselves. God sends people into their lives who will aid them in their efforts, but these people will not force our addicts into recovery or into a recovery program. What they will do is to insist that our addicts take responsibilities for their own actions, and these people will also hold them accountable for what they do and say.

Since addicts in recovery need to work their own programs, they certainly do not need their families to work these programs for them. We are often tempted to take over for our addicts and exert our own control over their recovery efforts. We may have done this in the past by enabling them, but we must step back in their recovery programs and let our addicts take over. If we fail to do this, we only hinder our addicts from getting help.

We want so desperately to "fix" our addicts that we will do anything to offer them assistance. Our addicts must yearn for recovery just as much as they desire their addictions. The addict in my family often related to me that he would go out of his way to get alcohol. So, in the same way, he must put the same effort, time, and dedication into his program of recovery. He has often said to me, "I was dedicated to the drink, and I must be dedicated to sobriety." I can recall an incident in his early efforts at sobriety. His sponsor at the time had asked him to attend a meeting one evening. It was pouring down rain outside, and my loved one was reluctant to go out in such messy weather. His sponsor reminded him that he would not have hesitated for one moment when he was drinking to get in his car and go out to secure alcohol, even if it was pouring rain. His sponsor challenged him to take his recovery as seriously as he had his drinking.

We must turn our addicts over to God and take the risks that there are other people more qualified than we are to help our addicts. Turning our addicts over to God and people that God sends into their lives shows our dependence and trust in God. We believe that God will lead our addicts each day. We should constantly pray for them, asking God to provide them with the strength to be faithful to their recovery programs and strength so that they can resist the temptations to resume their addictions. Yet, we must allow their sponsors to guide them in recovery and not interfere as family members. We also must not constantly remind them to call their sponsors, because when we do this, we are taking over and controlling their programs for them.

We fear our addicts will relapse. So we find it our bounden duty to constantly watch them every waking moment. God does not want us to live with this nagging uncertainty. In addition, our addicts will often resent our efforts at not allowing them any privacy as we stand guard over their lives. We create tensions and strained relationships with our addicts when we intrude into their recovery programs. We also display our lack of trust in our God, because we lack the willingness to submit our addicts to God and others.

When we turn our addicts over to the care of God, we allow our loved ones to accept certain responsibilities. These responsibilities include attending recovery meetings, talking daily with their sponsors, praying to God each day, reading recovery materials, working on their relationship with God, and reaching out to others in service. They need to develop or renew a spiritual relationship with God that has often been diminished or lost during their period of addiction. The spiritual aspect of their recovery program will be the most important part. Many addicts will tell us that they have tried for years to become clean, but nothing seems to work. A spiritual program of recovery leads the addicts to turn their will over to God and recognize that their lives have become unmanageable.

The addict in my family strived for years to work a program of recovery but without success. He was in and out of treatment centers and recovery meetings. Finally he found a sponsor who required him to work on his spiritual relationship with God. This sponsor asked him to pray every day, morning and night, and to do so on his knees. Getting on his knees was humbling, and it helped him to realize that he was not in control of his life. God directed his life as long as he was willing to submit to God's leadership.

Every day now, he wakes up and reads devotional materials particularly designed to help him confront the disease of alcoholism. These readings offer him guidelines to prevent relapse, and they increase his spiritual growth as a child of God. The materials remind him of the selfish nature of alcoholism, but they also affirm his self-worth. His sponsor also requires him to call other addicts in his recovery community so that he recognizes the importance of a caring community that is faithful in its members' concern for him. The community is filled with individuals who are willing to hold him accountable for his actions. In turn, he reaches out to other alcoholics, holding them accountable for *their* deeds. His focus, in giving to others, is to help the alcoholic in need, but as he serves others, he finds that his own spiritual life is strengthened. Working a sincere program of recovery is demanding, but anything less can cause our addicts to relapse.

This type of dedicated spiritual program is essential for my addict in his recovery, just as it will be vital for the recovery of other addicts. My loved one related to me why this spiritual aspect of his program of recovery was so important. In his state of alcoholism, he says he had "crossed over from human aid." He was so dominated and controlled by the disease of alcoholism that human aid was not enough to help him. By this he did not mean that others such as his counselors, sponsors, and those in his recovery community could not reach him. However, he needed much more than human help. He needed the spiritual dimension of a strong faith in God that would carry him forth in recovery because the evil forces of addiction had too great a hold upon his life. He did not reject the help of others, but he relied primarily on God and the spiritual tools of his recovery program.

There may come a time when it seems to many of us as if our addicts have lost interest in their families and their homes because of their recovery lifestyles. Our addicts make new friends and almost always have to reject friends who remain in addiction. They must attend meetings daily, a pattern that they will need to continue for the rest of their lives. This places a strain on many families, who now vie for the time and attention of their addicts. It is easy for jealousy and resentment to make their way into our family life. Families must not harbor jealousy and resentment toward the recovery program and must honestly face the truth that recovery will, most likely, take our addict away from the family. Our addict's time will be consumed in attending meetings, working with sponsors, attending recovery events, and engaging in service projects. If we want our addicts to remain clean, we must come to an understanding as families how important and essential these things are for them. We may not like it, but the fact is that recovery must come first as the addict's number-one priority. Many times we will take a back seat to our addicts' recovery programs, and this is the way it must be.

Spouses of addicts have to possess a great deal of patience and bring to their marriage much understanding when their addicts are working a recovery program. Couples should sit down together and discuss the realities of recovery and what it might entail in terms of their marriage relationships. Spouses and addicts alike must compromise in order for recovery to be successful. Perhaps the addicts might agree to a certain day of the week that will be designated as a "date night," with undivided attention given to the spouse. Spouses of addicts should make every effort to attend family functions of the recovery community. This will allow spouses to have contact with other spouses of addicts and also give them greater understanding and appreciation for what their addicts are achieving in recovery. Addicts should also be supportive when spouses need to attend their own support groups or wish to seek counseling.

Children often feel neglected and ignored when one or both of their parents decide to enter recovery. Their parent is no longer able to spend as much time with them as in the past. Family rituals may be cast aside, rituals that were meaningful to the children, but which the recovering parents are forced to ignore. Children need security and routine during times of change, so the parent who is not in recovery must work diligently to provide this for the children. Addicts must be sensitive to the needs of their children and carve out quality and quantity time to share with them. Children should also be welcomed to attend family events of the recovery community where they can meet and interact with other children who face similar situations in their lives. Parents must work together to uphold traditions of the family or to create new rituals to replace those that may have to end due to recovery.

God gave us families so that we could love and support one another in mutual relationships. Recovery can disrupt the harmony of family life. Families who sincerely love and care for one another can find creative ways to allow their addicts to engage in recovery efforts yet also maintain family closeness. Keeping the channels of communication open in family life helps members to be able to express freely how they are feeling. An honest, affirming discussion about recovery issues as related to family life can keep the lines of communication open for all members of the family.

We often use the word "balance" when referring to our efforts in life to juggle all of our responsibilities and still keep a semblance of order in family life. For our addicts, however, "balance" can often be a code word for relapse. Addicts must give priority to their recovery programs. When they begin to practice balance, they soon learn that they are edging closer and closer to relapse. Their families are important to them, but recovery must come first. Many families who fail to understand this end up making unrealistic demands upon their addicts. We did not anticipate this circumstance, but this is the reality of what it means to live with a recovering addict. Only with God's help are we be able to remain strong and supportive for our addicts. We have already made numerous sacrifices, but recovery will demand even greater sacrifices than most of us have realized.

This seems unfair to us because we are the ones who are damaged also by the addictions of our loved ones. We stood by our addicts, and now we complain that we deserve better treatment. We did not bargain for this. We must pray to God to help us overcome the resentments and anger we may feel toward our addicts when they neglect us because of their recovery programs. We rejoice and thank God that they are in recovery and remember what shattered lives they lived prior to this time. We never want to go back to the past, even if we realize that the present and future mean we must give our addicts the freedom to grow and change. Changes are hard on families, especially when they have been put through so much upheaval. Our addicts do not love us any less because they must spend enormous amounts of time and energy on their recovery programs. It takes a great deal of courage to do what they are doing, and we must never hinder their positive achievements by our resentments and jealousies. We should be proud of our addicts' new life in recovery and let them know this by our compliments and support.

Sometimes addicts must remove themselves from their past environments in order to become successful at recovery. While this is difficult for family members, it is the only way some addicts can survive. Often this may happen when our addicts enter a treatment program. If given an option, they may decide to travel to a treatment center to stay until they complete their initial recovery. If our addicts choose to seek help outside of our geographic location, we need to understand that they will be making new friends and having new experiences that do not include family members. There will be many times during which we will have to reach out and trust God to take care of our addicts. We will also need to ask God to help us alleviate jealous or hurt feelings when we are not included in the happenings in our addicts' lives. Our controlling and enabling in the past now makes it challenging for us to release our addicts. We must seek God's help to let go of our addicts by giving them the independence and freedom required for growth.

Spouses of addicts find it difficult to have their partners living away from them, even for a short period of time. The absence of a spouse can place a strain upon the marriage and can lead to divorce in some cases. Spouses should make every effort to communicate regularly with their spouses as allowed by the treatment centers and make visits as often as possible. The spouses of addicts can be especially resentful of the addict's recovery program, as the demands of the programs leave the non-addicted spouses responsible for all of the child-care issues. Spouses should seek out help from family members and friends, and also rely upon help from their faith communities. Children should be given permission to contact their parents in recovery. Separation is never an easy time for any family, but hopefully spouses will realize that getting their addicts into a quality recovery program outweighs the strain of their absences and is worth the sacrifices on the part of the family.

The addict in recovery will be a different person than the one living in addiction. The spouse may find he or she is married to a very different person. The spouse who is accustomed to making decisions for the family may find that role challenged, and a husband or wife no longer dependent on an enabling spouse may suddenly not offer the enabler the satisfaction of being protector, caregiver, or martyr.

Of course, some addicts do not have the choice of long-distance recovery if they have family and job responsibilities that prevent them from leaving where they currently live. Living in the same communities where their addictions occurred can be very challenging for most addicts. Seeing certain familiar places and people can trigger old habits of addiction and make it harder for our addicts to retain sobriety. God calls us to be especially sensitive to our addicts who remain in the same environments and are now trying to work programs of recovery. Sometimes driving by a location can bring to mind memories of using drugs at a particular spot. We might help our addicts by not driving by that spot, at least when our addicts are in early recovery.

Alcoholics need for us to discontinue drinking in their presence, even if we are only social drinkers and have a few drinks now and then. We must remove all bottles of alcoholic beverages out of the house, because these can be temptations. Some alcoholics will tell us that once they are truly working their programs of recovery, they can be exposed to alcoholic beverages without negative consequences. However, out of respect for our recovering addicts, we should do everything in our power to help them. We also honor their efforts at recovery when we do not allow others to drink or carry out destructive behaviors in their presence.

We are not doing this because we want to baby our addicts or look upon them as helpless creatures. Rather, if our addicts have invested their whole selves into a rigorous program of recovery, we want to sacrifice for them out of love and to honor the efforts they have made, which have not been easy. God will give us wisdom and insight into ways we can help our addicts. When the addict in my family was in early recovery, we tried to be very sensitive when we entered a restaurant that served alcoholic beverages. There were many times when we asked the hostess to seat us in an area that was away from the bar. It was not that we did not trust our addict, but out of respect for him and his program of recovery, we desired not to sit and make our addict stare at the bar. We also knew that early in his recovery, it would be very difficult for him to be in such a setting.

If our recovering alcoholics tell us that they do not wish to enter an eating establishment that serves alcoholic beverages, we should honor this request, no questions asked. If our recovering drug addicts relate to us that they cannot be around acquaintances who still use drugs, we should not make them feel guilty for severed relationships. This must take place if our addicts wish to remain clean. If our recovering gambling addicts advise us that it is unwise for us to go on vacation to a spot where they previously gambled, we need to select another destination. This shows our addicts that we sincerely appreciate the efforts they are making toward recovery, and we never wish to violate their trust with unkind actions that make them uncomfortable.

Families must recognize how difficult holidays are for the recovering addicts in their families. Holidays will often intensify the guilt that our addicts carry with them, because they remember how their addiction spoiled family holidays in the past. We must remember how vulnerable our addicts are to relapsing during the holiday seasons. The addict in my family did not choose to come home during the holidays for some time because of this very problem. He chose to stay in his recovery community where there were many people who surrounded him with support during the holidays. If our addicts live at home with us and in our same geographical area, we should encourage them to seek out the support of their friends in their recovery communities during the holidays. We must give them freedom to miss some of our family gatherings so they can attend support meetings and take part in events of the recovery communities. If these recovery events are family-oriented, we should be willing to attend with our addicts, even if this breaks into our traditional family gathering. We may find we have to create new traditions in the family to help our addicts in their recovery.

One of the best ways we can help our addicts is to make sure they are in treatment centers that help them rather than hinder their efforts at recovery and treatment. Most addicts need ninety days or more in treatment centers for effectiveness. It takes this long for the body to begin to heal and the brain to begin to rewire itself, independent of the abuses of addiction. Some addicts can recover from a thirty-day program, but the chances of success are much greater if the program is ninety days or more. The more time one can spend in recovery, the more time the body has to heal itself and the more time the addict has to gain the tools needed for sobriety.

We can help our addicts by researching treatment centers that focus on our addicts' specific needs. If our addicts have dual diseases such as alcoholism and an eating disorder, we need to encourage them to attend a treatment center that specializes in these diseases. Some addicts need treatment centers that deal with an addiction along with a mental illness. Advertising as a dual diagnosis center does not necessarily mean that a treatment center is equipped to deal with mental illness along with addiction. Families must be very careful when selecting a treatment center for their addicts. This is a part of the responsibility that God entrusts us with, and we should take great care in our research and selection process. This requires a great deal of prayer and the guidance of the Holy Spirit as well as our God-given gifts of reasoning and common sense.

Eventually, that long-awaited day in our addicts' recoveries will come when they will be asked to make amends to us for the things they have done wrong in the past. Most programs of recovery encourage addicts to reach out to the people they have wronged in the past, and family members are at the top of the list. When our addicts come to us with their apologies, we should let them make these to us and not brush them aside or make excuses for their past behaviors. Often we are so happy just to have our addicts show the least bit of remorse that we want to forgive them without their having to say, "I am sorry." We must let our addicts make amends to us. They need to do this in order to remain sober and work their recovery programs. When our addicts come to us, we must listen patiently and thank them for their sincerity.

When the addict in my family came to us recently to make amends, he asked us what he needed to do to seek our forgiveness. We told him that we had already forgiven him and that God had forgiven him also. We reminded him that he was a beloved child of God. What we asked him to do for us was to continue working his program of recovery, to keep sober, and to reach out in service to others. What more could we ask of him than this? Each family must decide how they will react when their addicts come to them to make amends. However, we should let God guide us to find the right words that will affirm our addicts rather than tearing them down. As bitter as we may be and as justified as we may be in criticizing our addicts for what we believe are unforgivable past actions, we must learn to forgive them. Only God gives us the ability to forgive. He prepares us as we come to that time when our addicts wish to make amends to us for past mistakes.

One of the hardest things that my family has faced in recovery is recognizing that the addict in our family would not be coming home to live with us or in our same geographical area. Our addict chose to remain and live in his recovery community, a great distance from the place where we now reside. When he made this decision, we agreed to support him, even though it meant that we would not see him as often as we wished. As hard as it was, we had to turn him over to God and to his recovery community, knowing that this was the best way for him to remain sober. Even if others do not have to make this same type of decision, there will be other choices along the way in recovery requiring family support. As families of addicts, we need to seek God's help in all of these challenging pieces of recovery. As long as our addicts are not resuming their addictions and are not engaging in destructive behaviors, God obligates us to be supportive as family members because families are called to love and care for one another. Our support is possible only as we reach out to God to provide us strength.

If recovery for our addicts entails their separation from us, we must accept this as God's will for our addicts. God leads our addicts to the exact places where they may obtain the right help. We dare not step in and hinder our addicts for our own selfish reasons.

For some families, this means we provide financial support so that our addicts can enter a quality treatment center. We accept our responsibility to make sacrifices that deplete our financial resources. Seeking the help of trustworthy financial advisors helps us plan ahead for the future and helps us ensure we have adequate funds to assist our addicts. Some of us dreamed of purchasing some items that we now have to put on hold or taking vacations that we now have to forgo in order to offer financial support to our addicts. We may be filled with resentment toward our addicts when we realize that our money is being poured into treatment centers instead of going to provide for our future. Some of us have spent endless amounts of money in treatment centers, only to have our addicts relapse time and time again.

While we cannot go into bankruptcy to help our addicts, each family must discern, with God's help, how much financial support is realistic. This is a matter requiring serious prayer. Our financial advisors can guide in ascertaining how much money we can realistically allocate to our addicts in their recovery programs. A time may arrive when we are advised to be selective in giving out our funds or even to say no. When this happens, we must not feel guilty, but we must realize that we did all we rightly and fairly could, within our means, to provide for our addicts. Now they must shoulder some of the financial responsibilities. God grants us the wisdom to continually weigh and balance how much we allow our addicts to fall back on us financially. Eventually, we hope that their own employment opportunities allow them to wean themselves from us financially, but we must accept the face that this may be a long process.

Competent treatment centers require our addicts to secure places of employment before they are released into the community. Depending on where our addicts choose to live and the costs they incur, we may need to provide some financial assistance. Offering the addict in my family financial assistance so that he could continue to live in his recovery community—a city with a high cost of living—is not just a financial matter for my family but a matter of faith as well. We trusted my addict to continue to be diligent in his program of recovery. We told him that we would support him as long as he dedicated himself to diligently working a strong recovery program. Each family will have to decide, with God's help and with the knowledge of trusted financial advisors, the level they are willing and able to aid their recovering addicts financially.

Sometimes our addicts ask us to attend recovery meetings with them if their recovery communities allow us to be present. Attending such meetings provides a means for us to offer our support and to hear the stories of other addicts. These programs may be the first time family members are able to confront one another openly and honestly about the effects of addiction on family life. Attending these sessions shows our addicts that we are serious about their recovery and our own as well. Always check first to see if recovery meetings are open to the public, as many times there are closed meetings where only addicts are allowed to attend.

Many of the things we do to help our addicts in recovery stem from our belief in a God who does not give up on us, but who offers us grace in our time of need. Helping and supporting our addicts does not mean that we have forgotten the horrors of addiction, but we do pledge to support them as long as they stay in recovery. There are consequences to their actions, and we will not tolerate their addictive behaviors. But we will offer them forgiveness and grace, just as God offers us forgiveness and grace. We will extend to them these gifts as long as our addicts are sincere about their programs of recovery.

Having vowed to help our addicts as much as we can in their recovery efforts, there are also some things we must avoid when our addicts make the decision to seek help for their addictions. It is very easy for families to fall into the traps of unhealthy habits when our loved ones are in the recovery process. First, it is necessary to state very clearly to our addicts any boundaries or rules that we are setting as a family while they are in recovery. This is especially helpful and important if our addicts remain in our homes during their recovery period. If you wish for them to inform you when they leave the house for their meetings, let them know. We must set rules and stick to them.

However, we should not set unreasonably high expectations. Families often feel anxiety when their addicts are clean for some time, as they are constantly worrying about relapse. Asking our addicts to assume so many responsibilities that they are overwhelmed is not helpful. We must evaluate each addict's abilities, time constraints, financial situations, and family dynamics before imposing rules. When the addict in my family entered recovery and was able to secure a job, we discouraged him from returning to school at that time. We felt that he needed freedom to begin his job and attend his recovery meetings without the additional burden of school. Later on, however, we expected him to return to his coursework, and he agreed to this plan. Since my loved one lived some distance from us, another rule that we asked him to abide by was to call us frequently so that we would know how he was doing.

Each family must set their own rules and responsibilities for their addicts, depending on their family situations. Once we set these down, however, we must be sure we enforce them and not back down. As our addicts progress in their recovery programs, we will find that we are able to restore some of the trust that has been lost when our addicts were in the throes of addiction. Just as we learn to trust God to guide and direct our addicts, we must also begin to regain trust in them and their relationship with us. This takes time, and we should not be so vulnerable and innocent that we overlook ways in which our addicts continue to violate our trust. Yet, as we notice our addicts making process in their recovery programs and maturity in their own lifestyles, we can open up and gradually begin to trust them. We should not be naïve, though. We must recognize that addicts take a long time to develop habits of maturity, so we must pray to God for patience and understanding.

Recovery is, in a sense, like the journey of faith. Addicts take steps forward and steps backward. One day we are encouraged about the changes we see taking place, and the next day our addicts are back into their old manipulative ways of acting and thinking. This is normal for addicts, and we may see these patterns repeat themselves for some time, even years. Just as God is loving and patient with us as we mature in our faith, we must extend grace to our addicts. Recovery is a day-by-day process and we, along with our addicts, will make many mistakes. We must not be too hard on either our addicts or ourselves.

Another thing to avoid in recovery is allowing our addicts to manipulate us, especially when they are in the early stages of recovery. If our addicts are in treatment centers, they are expected to abide by the rules of the facilities. Most centers will not allow addicts to call home for a few weeks. When our addicts are given permission to speak to or visit their families, they will sometimes use this as a means of manipulation. They will complain that they are being treated unfairly or required to attend group or individual counseling sessions that they think are unnecessary. Some may try to persuade us to send them additional money, provide them with their car, or even come and take them home before they have completed treatment. We must be careful not to fall for the traps and excuses our addicts will use to convince us that we should help them break the rules.

Addicts are wonderful manipulators. Just being in recovery does not prevent addicts from reverting to their old patterns of making us feel guilty when we refuse to cater to their demands. We must ask God to give us strength to lovingly say no to our addicts' manipulative efforts. If we give in, we damage the work that has already been done by the professionals at the treatment centers who are attempting to lead our addicts in the right direction. We should allow them to do their work without our interference and without manipulation by our addicts.

If we sincerely love our addicts and earnestly desire for them to maintain sobriety, we must let them work their recovery without our interference, but with our unselfish support. Family support is extremely important and aids in the ability of our addicts to stay clean and sober. Supporting our addicts may include financial support, attending meetings with them, going together to professional counseling, or giving them our permission to live away from home in a recovery community. It can also mean attending family support groups at treatment centers, learning all we can about the diseases of addiction, and sacrificing time with our addicts so they can attend meetings and support groups.

We must rely upon our faith when our addicts are in recovery. This entails asking God to help us not to be jealous of the time our addicts spend with their sponsors or their friends in recovery. It may mean making sacrifices that we had not planned on making, in order to help our addicts achieve a life of sobriety. Whatever it takes, we must support our addicts in recovery and realize that recovery is a lifetime process. Our addicts must work on their recovery all of their lives, and as hard as it is, we must not stand in the way. This will require us to dig deep within ourselves and muster all of the resources that God provides us. We must be people of courage and fortitude. God expects us to put forth our best efforts. Of course, we will make mistakes along the way. However, when we do, we accept God's forgiveness and ask the forgiveness of our addicts and begin again. We also have to forgive our addicts, because they will also make mistakes on this difficult journey of recovery.

Families of addicts owe it to themselves to enter recovery. We are greater sources of strength for our family members and our addicts when we recognize that addiction has depleted our energy and strength. Addiction has left many of us drained of our spiritual resources and weakened in our relationship with God. Recovery allows us to care for ourselves. We yearn for this self-care, but we fail to seek it while we are so busy caring for the needs of our addicts.

We can begin a program of recovery by reading devotional materials that are designed for the families of addicts, using these helpful materials along with our daily Bible readings. We can read materials that help us to understand the disease of addiction. Audio or video materials are also helpful. There are support groups in the community that meet at least weekly, where families of addicts can gather and share with other people who have faced addictions in their families. Some of the community groups are designed for teenagers who have family members with addictions. A Web site listing for several of these groups is offered at the end of this chapter.

One of the lessons we garner from our addicts is the importance of giving to others as a part of our recovery programs. Addicts learn in recovery that they must be willing to reach out to others in order for their sobriety to work. Addicts remain self-centered if they do not serve others who are struggling as they once were. A part of their recovery is to give back to the recovery group by taking an active role in helping other addicts and making themselves useful in their recovery community.

Families who have given and given to their addicts often believe it is impossible to give anymore. Our first steps toward recovery come when we take care of ourselves. Only then are we able to begin to serve others. Our faith communities are always in need of our services, and we can be a source of help to families there who may have issues with addiction. Depending on how much we decide to reveal about our history of family addiction, we can help our faith communities begin to understand the nature of the disease of addiction. We can become advocates in our churches for allowing recovery groups to use our facilities, as well as spokespersons for workshops and educational events that help church members gain better understanding of addictions.

Our faith has taught us to be generous givers. When addiction strikes our families, we become so centered on our addicts that we forget how enriched our lives become when we share with others. We receive many blessings and joys from giving ourselves in Christian service. Addiction allowed us no freedom to escape the constant watching-over and caring for our addicts. When we accept recovery for ourselves, we are set free to make a real difference in our world. We are amazed at the ways God will open up doors of opportunity for us and will bring people into our lives who need to hear our message of hope.

Our addicts must work a program of recovery throughout their lifetime and so must we. Just as our addicts will never be cured of the disease of addiction, neither will we be cured as family members. Our recovery programs must be valuable enough that we will continue them and not give up. We may have to make changes from time to time, because as we grow in recovery, we experience unique challenges. We must be flexible and adapt to new ways of looking at our addicts, others, and ourselves. We learn some valuable lessons when we fully embrace our future in recovery.

Healing and rebuilding our lives takes time. There is no easy formula. Along the way, we will be challenged on ways to rebuild communication with our addicts. Learning how to be honest with our addicts is vitally important. We related to our loved one that, although we continued to love and support him, his addiction has affected our lives in certain ways. We clearly defined these ways for him: stress in our marriage, worry about his health, anxiety that his addiction would kill him, and financial loss. We build greater bridges with our addicts when we begin to trust them and can share our own hurts. When our addicts approach us to make amends for the past, we have to be accepting, loving, and supportive. We must relearn how to live in our families without the presence of the addictions that have taken up so much of our time and efforts. Our addicts teach us to be cautious and aware that we can relapse, just like our addicts, when we fall back into our old ways of thinking and doing.

If our addicts do not embrace recovery and work a diligent daily program, the "evil spirits" of addiction will return to their houses much stronger and more destructive than before. The same is true for families of addicts. We should not only clean house from top to bottom, but we must also replace the demons of addiction with the powerful tools of recovery. Recovery is hard work, and it is serious business. Only our best efforts will produce the results that can lead us forward toward a productive life. Only by turning our unmanageable lives over to a God who can partner with us to provide us the spiritual resources we need will we be successful. Then we also will find true peace and serenity. We cannot and do not have to make this recovery journey on our own. Our efforts, as good as they may be, are not enough to restore us to sanity. Prayer, worship, Bible readings, meditation, and service are all important tools we can use to help us along the way. Ultimately, though, we have to turn to God for our strength and guidance.

When we try to depend solely upon ourselves to work a program of recovery, we are likely to fail every time. We need others to pray for us and support us on this journey. We can reach out to trusted friends and other families who have also faced addiction. But our greatest source of comfort, trust, and power comes from the God who walks this journey with us. We are not alone. God holds us in His arms of grace. The Holy Spirit comes to bring us wisdom and discernment. Christ our Savior meets us on the road, offering us His example of suffering as our model of strength. This is a journey of courage. We are people of courage.

Girded with our tools of recovery and empowered with divine help, we tell the "evil spirits" to flee from us and never return to our "houses" again. They scamper away, reluctant to leave us, clinging to any morsel of our lack of faith. In the end, though, they leave our houses, for the light of recovery shatters the darkness of evil. Since evil cannot abide the presence of good, these spirits are forced into hiding. We must remember, though, that the evil spirits of addiction are always out there somewhere, in the shadows, lurking, waiting for us to deny our need for recovery. They are looking to enter our houses with an even greater vengeance. We cannot afford to ever let them in again. Our recovery program must fill that house with spiritual resources so there is no room for evil spirits to return.

Faith provides us the key to opening the doors of our houses to the fresh winds of change. At the same time, faith is also the only lock strong enough to keep out the evil spirits of addiction from once again invading our spiritual houses and destroying our lives. When our houses become the temples of the Spirit's dwelling, homes that are warmed by God's love and made clean by our recovery efforts, the evil spirits of addiction will skulk away, defeated by forces greater than their destructive powers. Thanks be to God.

Web Sites for Families and Addicts

Addicts

Alcoholics Anonymous Worldwide: *www.aa.org*

The Anxiety Disorders Association of America: *www.adaa.org*

Anorexia: *www.aad.org*

(National Association of Anorexia Nervosa & Associated Disorders—ANAD

Borderline Personality: *http://www.healthplace.com/*

(Dealing with other mental health issues as well)

Bulimia: *http://www.bulimiarecoveryblog.com*

Cutting: *http://www.sobercircle.com/group.aspx?groupID=176*

Depressive Illness: *www.depression.org*

Dual Recovery Anonymous: *http://www.dualrecovery.org*

Cocaine Anonymous: *www.ca.org*

Emotions Anonymous: *www.emotionsanonymous.org*

(Depression, anxiety, and compulsive behaviors)

Gamblers Anonymous: *www.gambleranonymous.org*

Marijuana Anonymous: *www.marijuana-anonymous.org*

Narcotics Anonymous: *www.na.org*

Overeaters Anonymous: *www.overeatersanonymous.org*

Sexual Addicts Anonymous: *www.sexaa.org*

Sexaholics Anonymous: *www.sa.org*

Sexual Compulsive Anonymous: *www.sca-recovery.org*

Sexual Recovery Anonymous: *www.sexualrecovery.org*

Shopping Addicts: *www.shopaholicanonymous.org*

Workaholics Anonymous: *www.workaholic-anonymous.org*

Rita B. Hays

Families of Addicts

Al-Anon Family Groups: _www.al-anon.org_
  (Twelve-step support for families of alcoholics)

Alateen: _www.alateen.com_
  (Support to family and children of alcoholics)

Codependent Anonymous: _www.coda.org_
  (Support to families with addictions)

Hazelden: Educational Materials: _www.hazelden.org_

Nar-Anon: _www.nar-anon.org_
  (Twelve-step support for families with addictions)

National Association for Children of Alcoholics: _www.nacoa.org_

CHAPTER TEN:

I Can't Do This Anymore!

> *"By the rivers of Babylon—there we sat down and
> there we wept when we remembered Zion. On the
> willows there we hung up our harps. For there our
> captors asked us for songs, and our tormentors asked for
> mirth, saying, 'Sing us one of the songs of Zion!' How
> could we sing the Lord's song in a foreign land?"*
>
> *Psalms 137:1–4 (NRSV)*

In 587 BCE, a devastating event occurred in the history of the nation of
Israel. The might and strength of the Babylonian nation was evident in their
powerful army, which swept in and swiftly conquered Israel. The people
were captured, and the victors quickly removed them from the familiar
comforts of home. They were exiled far away to a distant and strange place
called Babylon. This frightening event, along with the Exodus, was pivotal
in forming them as the people of God. In the midst of a culture that was
diametrically opposed to their way of living and worshipping, the people of
Israel attempted to retain their cultural and religious identity. Times were
hard, and the future was uncertain. The Babylonians ate different foods
and worshipped many gods. Their environment completely changed for the
people of Israel. They now lived in a strange land, with unfamiliar food,
customs, and religious mores. The people responded with the lament we
find in the book of Psalms. They wept when they remembered the past, and

they were heartbroken because they believed there was no possible way for them to lift their voices in praise of God in this unfamiliar land.

Families of addicts know what it is like to live in the land of exile. The captors of addiction have removed us from the any semblance of normality and placed us in a foreign world that is strange and unfamiliar to us. Addiction alienated us from our relationships with others, our relationships with God, and our relationships with our addicts. Misunderstandings about the nature of addiction caused many people, including some in our own faith communities, to ignore us, judge us, or alienate themselves from us, so we felt exiled to a foreign land. So, like the Israelites, we wonder if it is possible to "sing the Lord's song in a foreign land." There are times in our journey of addiction that we too hung up our harps of joy on the willow trees and refused to sing. Addiction has tormented us to the point that our joy has been reduced to sorrow. Like the people of Israel, we weep tears of sadness and regret as we remember what it was like prior to the time when addiction exiled us to a foreign land where we have been held captive.

Is there any hope for us in this strange land of addiction? Are we, the exiled, the captive, the families in addiction, ever going to be able to return to a place and time where we can release our hearts and souls from the terrible burdens we have carried and lift our voices in praise once again? Are we sometimes drawn, like Israel, to the temptation of giving up, to hanging up our harps on the willow trees, and letting addiction continue to be our captors? Or will we be able to rise up, stronger and more powerful people than before, and once again sing zealously the songs of Zion? For some of us, this picture of renewal and refreshment seems a long way into the distance, but as people of faith, it is the lens of expectation through which we must always be looking.

Letting go and allowing God to assume control of our situations proved to be one of the most difficult challenges in our addiction journey. Some of us have done this, and we have experienced the freedom that comes with releasing our addicts to God and to others. Some of us are still working toward this goal, and others are just beginning to consider the importance of letting go. We have not let go of our addicts in the sense that we have stopped loving them or viewing them as beloved children of God. We released them to recovery communities, or in some cases, released them to continue in their destructive behaviors so that we could seek help for ourselves. All of us, for our own sanity and recovery, let go of certain behaviors and attitudes. Doing so has instilled in us peace, serenity, and the opportunity to enter our own programs of recovery.

Some of the things that held us captive in the past we removed from our lives and replaced them with our programs of recovery and our sustained faith in God. Recovery forced us to change our attitudes of judgment we placed upon our addicts and their diseases. We continued to work on our compulsions to control our addicts and their recovery programs. Even our expectations of what the future holds are replaced with more realistic pictures. At one time, we had certain dreams for our addicts, which addiction easily shattered. Now we live with new dreams of a better day for them. We learned to live each day, one day at a time, being thankful for small steps of progress toward recovery in the lives of our addicts and our families. We are honest in admitting that our future remains uncertain. Recovery may or may not be in the picture for our addicts, but recovery is in our picture nevertheless. Some of our addicts will always be bound to the disease of addiction, and for this we are saddened. Yet we cannot and must not blame ourselves. We move forward with our own steps toward recovery.

In the past, many of us thought that if we prayed ceaseless requests, if we exhibited strong enough faith, and if we worked the program of recovery for our addicts, they would turn around and get better. Addiction clouded our way of thinking. We forgot how powerful and menacing is the disease of addiction. We still pray, but now our prayers are not only for healing and recovery for our addicts, but especially for strength to meet all the constant challenges that addiction brings along our paths. We are still people of faith, but our faith has been forged in the midst of difficult situations. We confess that at times our spirits are broken, our bodies are assaulted, and our minds are weakened, but we are still standing! We wobble at times under the pressures of addiction, but we still continue to get up, stand up, and hold our heads up high.

Lessons We Have Learned

We admit that in spite of our hatred for the addictions our loved ones endure, we have learned some valuable lessons along the way. One truth is that we did not cause this disease of addiction and we cannot control or cure it. We learned this lesson the hard way by trying to control and cure our addicts and by placing guilt upon ourselves when we thought perhaps we held some responsibility for our addicts' decisions. We learned to remove the guilt from our lives and also not to blame our addicts for their uncontrollable and unpreventable actions. Our addiction experiences taught us the hard lesson of forgiveness. Offering forgiveness to our addicts—especially when, in our hearts and minds, forgiveness was undeserved and unmerited—taught us of the forgiving nature of our God. We fought and struggled to learn the lessons of setting boundaries for our addicts, but we are growing in this area of our relationship with our loved ones. Our addicts still easily manipulate us, and it is tempting for us to cross the line between helping our addicts and entering the forbidden zone of enabling them. Against the selfish nature of addiction, we counteract by focusing on ourselves for the sake of our own survival. To be at all successful in the realm of addiction, we are forced to seek out and work diligent and dedicated programs of recovery for ourselves.

Addiction taught us how to live as selfish people who constantly centered upon the needs of our addicts. We ran ourselves ragged and depleted our spiritual resources when we spent enormous amounts of time focusing on their needs. Now we are beginning to understand that we must work on the spiritual aspects of our own lives if we are to have any hope of peace and serenity as families of addicts. We admit that addiction is a much greater power than we ever realized. We lived unmanageable, insane lives. Our contact with God stands as our fortress and remains vitally important as we seek recovery for ourselves. We discovered we needed a power greater than ourselves, a loving God who restored us to sanity.

We embraced the power of God's grace that is at work in our lives. We reached out to God in our prayer life and in our times of worship and meditation. We sought the strength that God provided us. What we discovered is that God was with us at all times in our addiction journeys, but often we stayed so centered on the uncontrollable situations of addiction that we ignored Him or failed to enter into an intimate relationship with our Maker. God continued to remain close by our sides, always faithful to us regardless of what happened in this uncertain, perilous journey of addiction. We cannot always be sure of what the future holds for us, but we can cling to our God who offered us and continues to offer us grace sufficient to meet whatever comes our way.

The addict in my family often reminds me that I need a power greater than myself to rely upon, and this cannot be just any power. When he first entered recovery, he was drawn to the teachings of his recovery community that he must diligently seek after a power greater than himself. His recovery community left this "higher power" open-ended so that all people of different religious backgrounds or of no religious persuasion might feel comfortable in the recovery program. However, what our loved one found was that not just any higher power would work for him. He needed and sought after a higher power in his Almighty God. He said, "My higher power could not be a doorknob; I needed God as my higher power." His addiction has been so forceful as a negative factor in his life and has yielded such a devastating blow upon his life that he could not settle for just any higher power. God had to be front and center in his life, and his greatest priority had to be his recovery.

In the same way, we now look to God as our higher power. We seek after God with all of our hearts, minds, and souls. We put God first in our lives and grab all of the resources that God provides us, including prayer and the empowering of God's Holy Spirit. We continue to listen to the Holy Spirit as God's Spirit directs us and offers us wisdom and discernment when we face difficult decisions. We find time for quiet and reflection that allows us to hear God speaking to us through the Holy Spirit. We ask prayerfully for patience and courage for the challenges that are ahead of us. Those of us who grab these tools of our faith find ourselves progressing in recovery.

Yet there still remain times when we believe that we have little faith to offer our God. The quantity of our faith is not what is important; it is the sincerity by which we come before our loving God. Our faith grows and develops as we draw closer to God, but we must approach Him with whatever measure of faith we now possess and let God have control of our lives. When Jesus's disciples asked that their faith be increased, Jesus did not judge them for their lack of faith. He did not condemn them for their doubts. He told them that if they had faith only the size of a mustard seed, that faith had the potential to grow into a large plant. God will take whatever size faith we offer to Him and begin to work in our lives to increase our faith each day.

> *"The apostles said to the Lord, 'Increase our faith!'*
> *The Lord replied, 'If you had faith the size of a*
> *mustard seed, you could say to this mulberry tree,*
> *"Be uprooted and planted in the sea," and it would*
> *obey you.'"*
>
> *Luke 17:5–6 (NRSV)*

Before addiction entered our lives, we defined faith in terms of what we believed. "Having faith" was merely religious language for wishful thinking, orthodox beliefs, or clinging to some ill-defined hope. That was before we encountered the miracle of recovery. Faith is now the lens through which we view the world. It is a world where God is at work, healing those who are sick with addictions, opening the eyes of loved ones who are blinded by drugs, or raising to new life the most pitiful and hopeless alcoholic.

Addiction taught us many lessons about relationships. We learned we cannot trust just anyone and that not everyone we meet understands or appreciates our situation. Some of us have encountered unfair judgment from others. Unfortunately, some of these individuals worshipped in our own faith communities. We learned painfully whom we can open up to with our family secrets and upon whom we cannot depend. Yet addiction has offered us the opportunity to educate many people about the nature of addictions. Some of us are beginning to see positive changes within our faith communities regarding the ways others view addiction. God opened up doors of opportunities for us to share and to help many families who struggle with addiction.

Addiction turned our loved ones into people we could not trust; for some of us, this trust has been reworked and reshaped as our addicts have entered recovery. We have faced experiences of getting re-acquainted with our addicts on a new level in terms of trust, responsibility, and accountability. This has taken time and patience, and for every step we take forward, we take steps backward and make many mistakes. Starting over in our relationships with our addicts has been a matter of trust. As we forged a new relationship with our addicts, we stopped and listened to the amends they offered us, not judging, but accepting these as sincere pleas for forgiveness. We are still vulnerable and naïve at certain points in our relationships, but we continue to grow and mature as we open ourselves to recovery.

Many of us once traveled our journeys of addiction in isolation from others, but we cannot make our journeys alone. God never intends us to live solitary lives bereft of the help and support of others who understand our plight. We need God's help, but we also need the help of fellow sojourners who understand what it is like to live as family members in homes where addictions are present. Opening up to others who have journeyed on the road of addiction helped us know that others have faced our same trials and problems. Addiction isolated us from others, especially those who can be the greatest sources of friendship and support. Reaching out to the resources in our community and to the people who empathized with us provided us a well of strength to draw upon when we lacked the energy or the motivation to continue along this hard path.

Realities We Face

We embarked upon a journey that has no end in our lifetime. Our loved ones will always be addicts, and we will forever be the family members of addicts. There are pitfalls we encountered and some our addicts faced, which can sometimes set us back in our efforts to move forward toward healing. If our addicts chose recovery, we still find that their confidence is shattered on occasions when they think they are making little progress in their recovery efforts. We can be encouragers during these rough periods without becoming enablers or controllers. We uphold them with fervent prayers and encourage them to seek help from their sponsors and friends in their recovery communities.

Most addicts come to a point in their recovery efforts where they reach barriers. In the first few months of sobriety, they may experience what addicts call a "pink cloud." This refers to euphoric feelings our addicts achieve in early recovery when they are clean and begin to sense a new direction in their lives. After this initial phase of giddiness and excitement wears off, the reality sinks in regarding the challenge of remaining on a steady path of recovery. The journey wears them down, and they become weary and discouraged. Thus, our addicts experience depression, gloominess, and anxiety. Some addicts cannot adjust, and they relapse during these times. When our addicts relapse, we must not judge them; rather, we need to support them and encourage them to pick themselves up and start over again.

As families of addicts, we can also experience a "pink cloud" if we are not realistic about our own recovery efforts. It is easy at the beginning of our own recovery journeys to become very excited about working on our problems. Often, though, commitments and responsibilities outside of recovery squeeze out the time we previously used for our recovery. Our recovery efforts take a back seat to the other priorities in our life. Also, we may find that the excitement and anticipation of working our programs of recovery dull with the recognition that our efforts entail hard work. Gradually we find ourselves forgetting about working our programs of recovery and relapsing into complacency about our need for even doing so. Like our addicts, we must be very careful to continually evaluate our own efforts at recovery and be aware of the "pink cloud" that can surround us as well.

Another barrier to recovery comes when our addicts who are single enter into dating relationships too quickly. Most recovery programs advise addicts not to engage in dating relationships until they are clean for at least a year. This seems like a long time to most of us, but addicts need time to discover who they are in relationship with others. If our addicts were in a serious dating relationship prior to beginning recovery, that relationship is often strained as the person who is the non-addict gropes to come to terms with the new person they are now dating. Addiction changes individuals, and recovery changes them as well. If we are married to an addict, we too can feel tensions within our marriage relationship once our addict enters recovery. The recovery becomes a priority for them, so we often feel left behind, outside of the new world our addicts have entered. When this occurs, resentments toward our addicts and their recovery programs can creep into our marriage. Some of us must avail ourselves of professional help, but all of us need to pray about our relationships and perhaps turn to our pastors and trusted church friends for advice.

Addiction cuts into our family lives in such a painful way that many of us wonder if we will ever experience happiness and peace again. We do have choices, however. God granted us free will, and we have the option to decide whether we will choose to heal or continue to sink further and further into the clutches of addiction. We did not choose addiction; it was thrust upon us before we knew what was happening. We have to accept the fact that this is our circumstance in life. We have been dealt an unfair hand, but that happens to individuals who live in an imperfect world filled with human beings who make unhealthy choices.

Accepting that addiction is always going to be a part of our family identity can be painful, but that acceptance also sets us free to devote our energies toward the healing process. Our lot in life may not be what we expected it to be or what we would have wanted it to be, but we must learn to accept the reality of our family situations. We cannot change the reality that loved ones in our families are addicts. What we can change is our attitudes toward our circumstances. God does not expect us to wallow in self-pity or self-imposed guilt. God has set us free so we can begin to explore avenues of healing that God can provide us.

Hope for Our Futures

We can move forward in our addiction journeys, but only when we turn our lives over to God, release our addicts to His care, and embark on a new journey of recovery for ourselves. God provides us choices in life. We can blame our addicts, put ourselves down, and refuse to admit that we need help as much as our addicts do. Alternatively, we can choose to quit judging our addicts for diseases they cannot control, stop heaping guilt upon our own heads, and recognize that we are as sick as our addicts. We can take positive actions toward healing for our family members and ourselves. We can decide that no matter how vicious the disease of addiction is, it will never defeat us, because we are strong people, secure in our faith. Our attitudes play a great part in whether we will face our situations with maturity or let addiction regain the upper hand. Nothing is fair about being saddled with the problems that addiction brings into family life. Life is often unfair, but life is still good. Life is a gift, and we can choose to live it with integrity.

At times, our problems seem overwhelming and our lives so chaotic that we simply want to give up. The problems continue to mount up—guilt, depression, loss, and all of the hurts associated with addiction. What we will learn over time is that we simply cannot deal with all of these issues by ourselves, but God is strong enough and powerful enough to take what we cannot do for ourselves and begin to work in our lives. God offers to provide strength for all of our piles of hurts, pains, guilt, and losses, and help us deal with them . We have to be willing to surrender these things to God and not continue to hold on to them as reminders of our failures and our weaknesses.

Think of the witness to our faith that we demonstrate when we face our problems with God's grace. Every day, we encourage people who may be struggling with faith issues. We hope they are encouraged when they see us living out our faith in spite of the difficulties addiction has brought us. Addiction is strong, but it is never stronger than our God. Addiction is an evil force, but God's love is greater. None of us would ever wish this horrible disease upon our family, but we must ask ourselves in what way God can use us to show God's love and mercy to those around us. Addiction enlarges our vision, giving us an awareness of what difficult challenges many people face every day. We can sympathize to a greater degree with the suffering of this world because we too have suffered greatly. God does not call us to shut ourselves up in our own little world and forget about others. We have a message to carry to the wider world. This message is that the love of God is far greater than the stronghold of addiction. God's grace is sufficient to meet our needs, no matter how terrible our circumstances in life.

God wants to use each of us to carry the message of His redemptive love for us. When we make ourselves available as vessels of God's grace, we will be surprised to find the people God will bring our way who need to have encouragement and hope offered to them. We are the very people God calls to show others that we refuse to let external circumstances dictate our faith in God. We remain faithful to God, despite what the world throws at us. We carry a message of hope.

Christian hope is not grounded in wishful thinking. Our hope is so much more than getting what we desired. What we desired was never to have had loved ones who were addicts. Our hope is that our addicts will change and begin programs of recovery. Yet, even if this never happens, we are still people of hope. Our hope is anchored on God's love for us and secured in God's grace that continually reaches out to us. Our hope falls into the biblical pattern of those believers who are faithful to God in spite of their situations in life. We see this time and time again in our biblical stories of faith. Many individuals in our stories of faith also dealt with unthinkable situations. They clung to their hope in a God who was faithful despite the outcomes. Our situations in addiction may get better as our addicts embrace recovery, they might remain the same, or they could become worse. Yet, our hope still remains in a God we can trust to guide us through whatever circumstances we face and to give us the strength to endure whatever life brings our way. Courage comes not from having our situations alleviated but from enduring and remaining steadfast in our faith. We witness to our strong faith in God when we encounter the painful and sad happenings in our life with grace and peace.

There is a difference between wishful thinking and hope in the accounts in our Scriptures. Wishful thinking means that we want our selfish desires to be fulfilled. We want instant gratification, and we become impatient when things do not work out the way we expected them to occur. Hope, however, is based upon our belief that God is at work in our lives in a powerful way. We are instruments of God, used by God to advance His kingdom here upon this earth. Hope does not disappoint. Addiction always disappoints us because it is self-centered and founded upon our addicts achieving their own desires and fulfillments. Feeding their addictive habits leads them to do whatever it takes to get what they want out of life.

Dealing with addictions in our family life can cause us to lose hope, because we are basing our hope on whether our addicts are able to rid themselves of their addiction. From now on, we must look at hope independent of whether our addicts claim recovery or not. Of course, we pray that our addicts will choose recovery over their addictive lifestyles. Yet our hope in God must not be dependent on whether our addicts change or not. Our hope is ultimately dependent upon our believing in God and trusting in Him to help us in the midst of our addiction journeys. Our hope springs from our trust in God to sustain us in spite of the whirlwind of our lives.

The apostle Paul also faced great suffering in his lifetime. He was beaten, imprisoned, and eventually martyred for his faith, but he remained certain of God's abiding presence with him. Like us, Paul daily faced his "thorn in the flesh." The Scriptures never identify for us what exactly this "thorn in the flesh" was for Paul, but we name our "thorn in the flesh" addiction. Regardless of what each of us faces in life, Paul admonished us in all circumstances to give thanks to God because this demonstrates our reliance on God for our source of strength. Not only this, but our suffering also produces within us the strength to endure. This, in turn, produces character, which turns into hope.

> *"... knowing that suffering produces endurance, and endurance produces character, and character produces hope."*
>
> *Romans 5:4b (NRSV)*

Given all we endured, we have difficulty looking beyond our suffering to find any good outcomes. We are often blinded by the unhealthy and destructive aspects of addiction. Yet, each of us should take a close evaluation of the positive ways our suffering has turned us into people of hope.

Even if we do not blame God, our addicts, or ourselves for our suffering, perseverance has not been an easy task. Yet we have endured, mustering up all the strength and courage we could to help us through very trying times. Yes, there has been much destruction in our home life. Relationships have been severed and much damage has been done, some of which might never be repaired. We do not wish to see a picture of suffering as a pious, detached part of our lives. Our sufferings were very real, immensely hurtful, and they have tested our faith to a degree to which it had never previously been tried. Yet, what Paul is telling us is that our suffering did produce some good after all. We did not suffer in vain. We would not wish our suffering upon others and ourselves, and if we had to do it again, we would not suffer just for the lessons we have learned. Paul wants us to know that suffering can have positive effects.

The writer of the biblical book of James goes even further to dare ask us to consider our trials as nothing but joy.

> *"My brothers and sisters, whenever you face trials of any kind, consider it nothing but joy, because you know that the testing of your faith produces endurance and let endurance have its full effect, so that you may be mature and complete, lacking in nothing."*
>
> *James 1:2–4 (NRSV)*

His declaration of faith seems absurd to us when we consider that we have experienced anything but joy in our addictive homes. Yet, we admit with the writer of James that our faith has been tested. God did not cause the addictions, and God is not using the addictions as a means of testing our faith. The testing comes with the attitudes and character we have displayed as people of God in the midst of our suffering. We have either shown others that we trusted and believed in our God to sustain us and carry us forward, or we have shown others our lack of faith and trust in God by giving up and resigning ourselves to our addictive situations without a fight.

Many of us have fought valiantly this endless battle of addiction, and regardless of the outcome, our faith has produced endurance to help us keep going and continue trying in spite of what happens to our addicts or to us. Some of us have fought a losing battle, seeing our addicts continue in their addictive lifestyles. Perhaps some of us have even witnessed our loved ones die from this awful disease, and we have faced sorrows that seemed too great to bear. Others of us have seen our addicts make progress and embrace recovery, but each day we live with the fear that our addicts will relapse. Yes, our faith has been tested in more ways than we can comprehend. Nevertheless, by our very endurance we have demonstrated a mature, growing faith that will not give up and will not be denied, even in the times of greatest misfortune.

We have learned the difference between happiness and joy. Happiness is often dependent upon external circumstances such as fulfilling jobs, material possessions, and the expectations of our lives taking shape into positive outcomes for us. When things do not work out the way we planned, we look upon these event and characterize them as unhappy times. Addiction left us facing some unhappy times in our lives. Yet, in spite of our unhappiness, we still carried forth with us the joy of the Lord if we are people of faith. Our lives, even in spite of addictions, consisted of burdens and blessings, healings and hurts, and successes and failures. We celebrated the blessings, healings, and successes. Our hurts, burdens, and failures still added up to joy for us because God took these pains and transformed them into perseverance. God took what was negative, ugly, and wasteful, and used those things to strengthen our faith. In spite of all of the bad and ugly, we are still left with great joy.

People who lack faith cannot begin to understand this kind of joy. Only believers, grounded in Scripture and prayer, and committed to walking each day with God, will appreciate and comprehend this kind of dualistic thinking. Amazingly, the writer of James tells us "to count it all" as joy. Count both the good times and the bad times as joy because of the work of God, who used all circumstances to transform our faith into even greater realms of maturity and joy. The writer of James is also telling us that the counting of joy does not happen until we face adversity. We cannot just include the blessings and victories of life and declare this as joyful. Troubles must be included as well! Joy is the product of pain and hardship, not the absence of it.

We are not talking about a silly, giddy type of joy where we plaster on a smile and project to the world that we are happy-go-lucky individuals who do not have cares or worries. Joy is a process that grows stronger as we allow God to strengthen our faith. Joy is the result of our faith in God in spite of our eternal circumstances. Joy is a gift from God, and we have to work at taking this gift and using it each day. Over time, we discover to our amazement that both the evil of addiction and the joy of our faith work together to produce joy.[1] The apostle Paul expressed this hope when he declared,

> *"All things work together for the good for those who love God, who are called according to his purposes."*
>
> Romans 8:28 (NRSV)

One of the greatest resources we have in Holy Scripture is to turn to the Psalms in our times of need. The Psalms are filled with many praises directed toward God, but they also contain many passages dealing with pain. The Psalms present us a poignant picture of steadfast suffering and agonizing pain, as our writers refuse to mince words but honestly address God. Reading the Psalms will tell us that it is possible to face the anguish of addiction without losing our faith. It is possible to discover joy even in times of suffering. It is possible to grow closer to God, even when our faith is tested by addiction.

The Psalms as Resources for Families of Addicts

Psalm 77

The author of Psalm 77 is Asaph, one of King David's chief musicians. Asaph has faced some great pain in his life, and he honestly and fervently pours out his heart to God.

> *"I cry aloud to God, aloud to God, that he may hear me. In the day of my trouble I seek the Lord; in the night my day is stretched out without wearying; my soul refuses to be comforted.*
>
> *Psalms 77:1–2 (NRSV)*

Like Asaph, as families of addicts, we have spent many sleepless nights pleading to God to help us. We have addressed our God with the same honesty as Asaph, knowing that we were beyond human aid and that God was the only one powerful enough to help us. As with Asaph, God seemed distant from us and we wondered if He was even concerned about our problems.

> *"Will the Lord spurn forever, and never again be favorable? Has his steadfast love ceased for ever? Are his promises at an end for all time? Has God forgotten to be gracious?"*
>
> *Psalms 77:7–8 (NRSV)*

Aspah came to a point in his life, as have many of us, where he questioned God. We wondered where God was in our suffering because we know that we could not bear the pain without the presence of our God. However, Asaph was able to move from a place of despair to a place of peace when he remembered God's faithfulness in the past. By recounting the wonderful deeds of God, Asaph was able to turn his sorrow into praise and his pain into joy. As we remember God's loving deeds and faithfulness to us, we too can begin to see God's hand at work in our lives, in spite of addiction. It helps us to list the ways in which God has been faithful to us and reflect upon God's great love and mercy to us in countless deeds of kindness.

> *"I will call to mind the deeds of the Lord; I will*
> *remember your wonders of old. I will meditate on all*
> *your works, and muse on your mighty deeds."*
>
> *Psalms 77:11–12 (NRSV)*

As we look at our lists and think how loved we are by our wonderful, gracious God, we too, like Asaph, can begin to praise God instead of complaining to Him. When we are in the grip of addiction and doubting God's faithfulness to us, it helps us to remember how much we are loved. Remember that God loves us with an unwavering love. Remember that God works to bring healing into our parched and dry lives. Remember that even in the dark times, God is present. Remember that just as God was faithful in the past, He will be faithful in the present and future. We need to remember and keep remembering.[2]

> *"Your way, O God, is holy. What god is so great as*
> *our God? You are the God who works wonders; you*
> *have displayed your might among the peoples. With*
> *your strong arm you have redeemed our people, the*
> *descendants of Jacob and Joseph."*
>
> *Psalms 77:13–15 (NRSV)*

Psalm 46

Psalm 46 declares that God becomes our refuge and strength in times of trouble. We can certainly relate to our need for a God big enough to help us in the situations we face. The psalm reminds us that God is "a very present help in trouble." God does not wait until our addicts have entered recovery to help us. God responds to our situations immediately. God never withdraws from helping us.

> *"God is our refuge and our strength, a very present help in trouble. Therefore we will not fear, though the earth should change, though the mountains shake in the heart of the sea; through its waters roar and foam, though the mountains tremble with its tumult."*
>
> *Psalms 46:1–3 (NRSV)*

The psalmist apparently faces some situations as devastating as ours. The writer does not fear, even if all of nature seemed to be in an upheaval. No doubt, these descriptions of the changes in the earth, the shaking of the mountains, and the roaring and foaming of the waters are metaphors for the chaotic situations that have impacted the psalmist. Like the writer of Psalm 46, families caught in addiction sense their lives being turned upside down with forces beyond their control. The psalmist invites us to dwell in the secure arms of God and not be afraid.

However, in order for us not to fear, we must quiet ourselves. We must shut off the constant babblings of our minds and the frantic fears of our hearts. Our tendency is to panic when we are uncertain which way to turn and what to do. When we are in the middle of the trap of addiction, our only healing alternative is to set aside our anxieties for the peace God brings us. Abiding in God's presence provides us with the solitude and peace we need to remove ourselves from the chaos of addiction. When the enemies of addiction come to taunt us, we must kneel before our God, trust in His ability to quiet our fears, and listen for Him to speak comforting words to us. This is difficult for families of addicts, because we resist being quieted in the midst of turmoil. When problems erupt, we are tempted to take control and resolve the situations with some type of action on our part. Yet God asks us to be still and listen for His message of hope to us.[3]

> *"Be still, and know that I am God! I am exalted among the nations, I am exalted in the earth."*
>
> *Psalms 46:10 (NRSV)*

Psalm 18

Psalm 18 echoes the message of Psalm 46 by letting us know that we can take refuge in our God, whom we can trust at all times. Our faith in God is established upon our past experiences with Him. We have known God to be dependable, trustworthy, and a God who keeps the promises made to us.

> *"I love you, O Lord my strength. The Lord is my rock, my fortress, and my deliverer, my God, my rock in whom I take refuge, my shield, and the horn of my salvation, my stronghold. I call upon the Lord, who is worthy to be praised; so I shall be saved from my enemies."*
>
> *Psalms 18:1–3 (NRSV)*

David, who is called by God to lead the nation of Israel, needs God's help at all times. He is assaulted, as we have been, by the enemies who threaten him.

> *"The cords of death encompassed me; the torrents of perdition assailed me; the cords of Sheol entangled me; the snare of death confronted me."*
>
> *Psalms 18:4–5 (NRSV)*

David finds himself in a hopeless situation, as we often do. David immediately turns to God for help because he believes in a God who is loyal and is a deliverer in his days of trouble.

> *"In my distress I called upon the Lord; to my God I cried for help. From his temple he heard my voice, and my cry to him reached his ears."*
>
> *Psalms 18:6 (NRSV)*

Given the kind of God David serves, David cannot help himself. He bursts forth into exuberant words of praise and worship. David provide us with a model of the ways we can proclaim the praises of our God regardless of our situations in life.[4]

> *"The Lord lives! Blessed be my rock, and exalted be the God of my salvation, … For this I will extol you, O Lord, among the nations, And sing praises to your name."*
>
> *Psalms 18:46, 49 (NRSV)*

Psalm 27

When the winds of addiction swirl around us, David invites us in Psalm 27 to run to God, fleeing into God's protective arms of love and grace. There is no fear in the presence of the Lord, because God comes to us bringing light and salvation. Addiction draws its power and strength from keeping us in a frantic and fearful state of mind. When God becomes the stronghold of our lives, the one we ferociously cling to as if our lives depended upon Him—and they do—then we proclaim the same assurance that David had that he would not be afraid of anyone or anything he encountered.

> *"The Lord is my light and my salvation; whom shall I fear? The Lord is the stronghold of my life; of whom shall I be afraid?"*
>
> *Psalms 27:1*

David does not exhort this kind of confidence in the Lord without drawing near to God for refreshment and spiritual nourishment. He humbly submits himself before God. He desires to learn the ways of the Lord. In the same way, we must desire to have contact with our God through intimate relationships of trust and humility. We must want to learn about how to follow God's will for our lives and seek His purposes for us at all times. David tells us that his enemies have gotten him off track and that he needs God to lead him on a level path. The enemies of addiction cause us to stray off of God's desired path for our lives. We affirm, along with King David, that we need to be led back in the right direction.

> *"Teach me your way, O Lord, and lead me on a level path because of my enemies."*
>
> *Psalms 27:11(NRSV)*

King David also reminds us of the importance of being patient and continuing to wait for the Lord to carry out God's work in our lives. Addiction causes us to become impatient. We would like to have the solutions to our problems immediately. We must submit our will to God's timing. This is difficult for us because we have lived as controllers and enablers. Now we must step back, humble ourselves, and become patient waiters upon our God. This takes courage, and we must be people of fortitude, as David expresses to us.[5]

> *"I believe that I shall see the goodness of the Lord in the land of the living. Wait for the Lord; be strong, and let your heart take courage; wait for the Lord!"*
>
> *Psalms 27:13–14 (NRSV)*

Psalm 63

Psalm 63 presents us with an interesting picture by David of our reliance upon God. David shares this psalm out of his experience in the wilderness of Judah. The wilderness, in biblical writings, is always the place where God forms and shapes us as His people. We remember the Children of Israel were forged as a nation through their wilderness travels, and Jesus came to a greater understanding of His messianic calling through the time He spent in the wilderness. Like those biblical sojourners, who learned great lessons from their wilderness journey, we too have found ourselves in the wilderness of life and have learned valuable lessons. David tells us that his soul thirsts for God because he is tired and worn out, just like many of us.

> *"O God, you are my God, I seek you, my soul thirsts for you; my flesh faints for you, as in a dry and weary land where there is no water."*
>
> *Psalms 63:1 (NRSV)*

David does not remain in solitary confinement, however. He goes into the sanctuary of the Lord to behold God's majesty. David does not tell us if he has entered the sanctuary of the Lord at a time in which worship is taking place or if he enters alone. However, there is something about being present in the sanctuary of the Lord that is appealing to David. In the sanctuary, David encounters God in a way that fulfills his soul. We also find solace when present in God's sanctuary. Addiction isolates us from others and seeks to destroy our faith. Relationships with other worshippers in our faith communities help us to remove our tendency to try to bear our burdens alone. We need the support and help of others. When we come into the sanctuary of the Lord in our places of worship, we enter into God's presence in a powerful way. Before us are all the symbols of our faith that tell whose we are and tell us who we are. Addiction's loud and clear message to us is that we are worthless, vulnerable, and weak. The symbols of our church tell us otherwise. They tell us that we are redeemed, holy, and beloved children of God. David longs to be in God's sanctuary, to behold God's glory and power, and we need to be in God's sanctuary to renew our spirits and remember our calling as the people of God.

> *"So I have looked upon you in the sanctuary,*
> *beholding your power and glory."*
>
> *Psalms 63:2 (NRSV)*

Psalm 63 was such an important psalm for the people of God that the early fathers of the church declared that not a single day should go by without the public singing of this psalm. Perhaps the church fathers understood, as we will when we read this psalm, that David has a common yearning for God after which we all seek. David craves to know God in an intimate personal relationship. David is fed by God's constant presence in his life, and he demonstrates this with praise. We discover that a part of David's ability to rely so heavily upon his God in the times of trouble and tribulation come from the intimate friendship that he had with God. This intimate connection enables David to cast his problems upon God. A part of our healing as families of addicts comes when we establish an intimate, close friendship with God through a disciplined prayer life, Bible study, meditation, and recovery program. Not only did David crave God, but David also found satisfaction in God. Do we crave God in the same way that our addicts crave their addictions and the exact way we feed into their desires with our constant enabling? Do we find satisfaction from being in the presence of God, and if so, do we offer our praises?

> *"My soul is satisfied as with a rich feast, and my*
> *mouth praises you with joyful lips."*
>
> *Psalms 63:5 (NRSV)*

David goes on to tell us that he literally clings to the Lord as if his life depended upon it. The Hebrew word *dabaq*, which translates in Psalm 63 as **cling**, literally means "to stick like glue." Given what we have gone through in our journeys of addiction, we must "stick like glue" to our Almighty God. It seems the problems of addiction have stuck themselves to us without our control and without our permission. Evil can readily stick itself to us if we are not careful to cling to our God. When we cleave ourselves to God, evil flees from us, unable to endure the presence of God. It cannot stand the light of God's love and desires only the dark places. Not only this, but David also assures us that God holds him and us with His right hand, that is, God's favored hand. God's favor rests upon us as it did upon King David. David goes on to tell us that he literally clings to the Lord as if his life depended upon it.[6]

> *"My soul clings to you; your right hand upholds me."*
>
> *Psalms 63:8 (NRSV)*

These are just a few examples of the rich heritage in the Psalms from which we can draw our strength as families of addicts. We have found ourselves in the valley of weeping. We may not be called out of our valleys, but God enters into the valleys with us, transforming our places of grief into valleys of blessing. Life is not easy when we find ourselves face-to-face with addiction, but we are blessed because we are in the presence of God, who walks closely beside us and sustains us. Our heartaches do not disappear, but we are blessed because God is faithful at all times. When we are weak, God makes us strong by becoming our very strength in time of need. When we fail to understand what is happening to us and why it is happening, we trust in God, because God's timing and purposes far surpass our limited vision. So we continue on our journeys, hiding in the shadow of the Almighty, clinging to the grace of God, and walking in hope. Not because our addictions have been removed from us, but in spite of them and because of them.

Our valleys of weeping become places of blessings when we recognize that our places of exile can be transformed with God's help. When the Children of Israel were torn from their homeland and taken into Babylonian captivity, they initially "hung up their harps on the willow trees" and refused to sing the Lord's song in a strange land. Sometimes we feel like doing the same, given our exile into addiction. Addiction robbed us of the comforts of home. Over time, however, the nation of Israel realized that if it were ever to survive it would have to draw upon its calling as a chosen people. The temptation was to negate one's heritage and convictions for the negative culture of Babylon. Israel could not afford to keep quiet about her distinction as a unique nation under God's leadership. The Jews of Babylon formed communities to preserve their heritage and their religion. Together they supported one another to show Babylon that they were different from the culture around them.

In the foreign land of addiction, in the unknown places to which we have been exiled, we must stand together as families of addicts. When we remain in solidarity, we show the world that we are not afraid because our God is with us. We need not hang up our harps and refuse to sing the Lord's song. Rather, we burst forth with songs declaring the praise of our God who offers us blessings in the midst of the barren wilderness of addiction. And we believe with all of our hearts that "Weeping may linger for the night, but joy comes with the morning" (Psalms 30:5b (NRSV)).

Facing the Unthinkable:

What if our situations never change or our loved one dies from addiction?

As unfathomable as it may be, we as families of addicts must face two unthinkable scenarios. *What if our addicts never seek recovery and remain in their addictions? What if our loved ones die from the disease of addiction?* In both situations, we ache for what might have occurred if addictions had not been present in the lives of our addicts. We know the potential of our addicts, and we grieve when we realize that their potential will never be realized.

We cannot blame ourselves for what happened to our addicts. If we do this, we will live with regret the rest of our lives. There is nothing we did to cause the addiction, and there was nothing we could do to cure or control our addicts. Our addicts were dealt an unfair disease that destroyed their lives and turned them into people we did not recognize. We did the best we could do in circumstances that were beyond our control and understanding. We need to take comfort in the fact that we are humans, and there are limitations to what we can do or control in life. Many factors in the disease of addiction fall into the category of "mystery."

Our loved ones rest always in the grace of God who created them as beloved children of God. We must never believe that God turned His back upon our loved ones. God always receives them into His loving arms and embraces them with His grace. No matter what our loved one has done, God remains forgiving. God understands far greater than we do about the conditions of our addicts and the struggles they have endured.

Our hurts are great, and our pains are very real. God grieves with us and sheds tears of sadness for us. God never abandons us in our grief, and He never abandons our loved ones to condemnation. He sends His Holy Spirit as a comforting presence in our lives at all times, but especially in our times of need.

As people of courage, we must move forward in our lives to seek recovery for ourselves. We do not forget our addicts. We continually pray for them and remember them as valuable children of God. We cannot allow them to keep us from seeking recovery for ourselves, however. Just as we have been admonished to turn our loved ones over to God in their addictive states, we are now called by God to release our addicts to the loving care of God. When they are in God's care, they are in the best possible place they can be. As difficult as it is, we release our addicts to God. Then we are free to embrace the light of a new day that is dawning just beyond the horizon of addiction.

When Christ our Savior was raised from the dead by the powerful act of God's resurrection, He neatly folded His burial clothes as if to say, "Thank you, but I do not need these anymore." When we experience God's resurrecting powers in our life, we toss aside the clothes of addiction that have bound us, come out of our tombs of despair, and enter into the light of a new day. This is the hope God offers us. For in spite of our deep losses and because of them, there is the hope of resurrection and new life for us. The stone is rolling away. Can we hear its grinding noise as it opens up the doors of new life for us? Can we believe it is actually rolled away now, so that we can emerge from the tombs of addiction into the light of the dawning of a fresh new morning? We want so desperately to believe. We do believe, but our sincere prayer is that God will help our unbelief.

Key Symbols of Our Faith as Signs of Hope in Addiction

The Message of the Symbol	The Message of Addiction
Anchor—We are anchored to Christ. We are secure in our faith.	Addiction seeks to anchor us to its forces of destruction, but Christ frees us.
Butterfly—Symbol of resurrection and new life.	Addiction offers us death and destruction.
Bible—God's Word that we turn to for guidance, peace, and strength. God's Word contains truth.	Addiction offers us no words of hope. Addiction lies to us and offers us no truth.
Candle—Christ is the light of the world and our hope.	Addiction wants us to live in darkness without hope.
Chalice & Cup—The broken body of Christ restores us to wholeness.	Addiction leaves us broken and shatters the peace in our lives.
Church—The community of God's people. We need our friends to support us and pray for us.	Addiction forces us to live in isolation. We turn away from friends and those who can help us.
Cross—Symbol of Christ dying to bring us salvation and to save us from our sins. We are set free!	Addiction convinces us that there is no way for us to be saved or released from its vicious clutches.
Dove—Symbol of the Holy Spirit. God's Spirit continues to abide with us, offering us peace, wisdom, and discernment.	Addiction is an evil spirit that wishes us only harm and no good.

Lamb—Symbol of Christ, the One Who gave himself willingly as a sacrifice for each of us on the cross.	Addiction sacrifices our families, our health, and our relationship with God on its altar of evil and destruction.
Shell—Symbol of our baptism. In our baptism, we are marked as beloved children of God.	Addictions marks us as weak, guilty, unloved, and unworthy people.
Shield—Symbol of God's protection and loving care.	Addictions leave us vulnerable and believing that no one cares about us.

Ways Churches and Church Members Can Help Families of Addicts

1. Be supportive, not judgmental.

2. Tell the families of addicts that you are truly sorry for what they are going through. Do not pretend that you understand what they are facing.

3. Be honest. Tell them if you have little knowledge of the disease of addiction and are willing to listen to their stories so you can learn.

4. Pray for the family.

5. Ask about how their addicts are doing.

6. Send them a card or call them from time to time to encourage them.

7. Allow support groups for families and addicts to meet in your church facilities and welcome these groups, but allow for their anonymity.

8. Hold workshops and seminars on addictions.

9. Educate church members about addictions as diseases.

10. Offer to help families with childcare needs.

11. Keep confidential anything they tell you that they ask you not to reveal to others.

12. Offer financial assistance for addicts in your church to attend quality treatment centers when families cannot afford the costs. Remember that some family members are embarrassed by their plight and do not necessarily want it known that they have an addict in the family. Have the pastor approach this family in a loving and confidential manner.

Ways Clergy Can Provide Support for Families of Addicts

1. Educate yourself to the aspects of drugs and addiction. Read materials from recognized sources such as Alcoholics Anonymous and Hazleden.

2. Keep books and resource materials in your office to make available for families of addicts and other church members.

3. Acquaint yourself with support groups in the community and research quality treatment centers so that you can assist church members.

4. Pray specifically for those caught in the grips of addiction. Pray in your private times of prayer, but also in the prayers of your faith community.

5. Mention the struggles that addicts face in your sermons when this is relevant.

6. Allow community support groups to meet in your church facilities.

7. Encourage family members of addicts to establish a support group within the community of faith to address certain issues.

8. Allow families of addicts to share with you, and be willing to refer them to counselors who are trained in addiction counseling.

9. Offer financial support to addicts who need to enter treatment programs but cannot afford the costs. Be aware that treatment centers are extremely expensive.

10. Be willing to attend some support groups in your community to learn about addictions. Visit only during designated "open discussion" meetings. Listen, but do not speak.

11. Pray for members of your faith community who are dealing with addictions.

12. Keep in strict confidence any secrets that family members share with you, as long as these secrets do not involve abuse.

13. Encourage family members who are dealing with addictions to seek help for family members.Get them involved in some aspect of service within the life of your congregation.

14. Remind your congregation that many people who face addictions also battle mental illness. Encourage your members to support such individuals non-judgmentally.

15. Explain to your church leaders that far more families are touched by addiction and mental illness than is commonly recognized.

Recommended Readings for Spiritual Growth

A Path through Suffering: Discovering the Relationship Between God's Mercy & Our Pain, Elisabeth Elliot, Vine Books, 1992.

The Blessing Book, Linda Dillow, NavPress, 2003.

God and Human Suffering, Douglas Jon Hall, Augsburg Fortress Publishers, 1987.

Making Sense Out of Suffering, Peter Kreeft, Servant Ministries, 1986.

Praying the Psalms, Thomas Merton, Liturgical Press, 1956.

The Problem of Pain, C. S. Lewis, HarperOne, 2001.

Psalms for Praying: An Invitation to Wholeness, Nan C. Merrill, Continuum, 2006.

The Psalms of David, James S. Freemantle & Stephen Freemantle, William Morrow, 1982.

Psalms, The Prayer Book of the Bible, Dietrich Bonhoeffer, Augsburg Fortress Publishers, 1970.

Reflections on the Psalms, C. S. Lewis, Harvest Books, 1964.

Sickness, Suffering, and Scripture, David Leyshon, The Banner of Truth Trust, 2008.

Suffering, Dorothee Soelle & Everett Kalin, Augsburg Fortress Publishers, 1975.

Suffering and the Courage of God: Exploring How Grace & Suffering Meet, Robert Corin Morris, Paraclete Press, 2006.

End Notes

1. Saundra L. Washington, "I Count It All Joy," 14 July 2005. *EzineArticles.com.* 28 March 2009. *http://www.ezinearticles. com/?I-Count-It-All-Joy&id=51261.*

2. Linda Dillow, *The Blessing Book,* (Colorado Springs: NavPress, 2003), 28–32.

3. Ibid., 48–57.

4. Ibid., 57–58.

5. Ibid., 58–60.

6. Ibid., 63–71.

Sources for Locating Treatment Facilities and Services

The heart of any recovery program for addicts and family members is a local support group within a larger recovery community. The various twelve-step support groups have national Web sites with searchable rosters of meetings by time, day of the week, and location; those same organizations provide toll-free numbers and often a local number available through any directory assistance service. Local social service agencies can also assist in finding a suitable group within a community.

At key stages in the recovery process, an addict may need more help, either in terms of medical assistance and counseling on an outpatient basis, or in the most advanced stages of addiction, the structure and guidance of a professional treatment center. The search for a nearby counselor experienced in addiction treatment can begin with one's health insurance company's Web site or from a listing at one's state licensing Web site; one independent database is found at *http://www.getmentalhelp.com*.

Finding a detoxification center or an outpatient service nearby is best done using the national database Substance Abuse Treatment Facility Locator maintained by the United States Department of Health and Human Services at *http://oasis3.samhsa.gov/*. Both public and private facilities are included, and a link to the agency's Mental Health Services Locator at *http://mentalhealth.samhsa.gov/databases/default.asp* is also provided.

While these locators are excellent for services near one's home, the search for an inpatient treatment center is more challenging. For instance, finding services by type at the national database for treatment facilities requires selecting "list search," then the appropriate state, then "select facilities ... according to services offered." One can then select the primary focus of the provider, type of service provided (halfway house, detoxification, etc.), and type of care. In the last category, some inpatient treatment centers will be listed as long-term residential (over thirty days), while very similar ones will be categorized as partial hospitalization/day treatment.

Given the number of entities in the national database, finding a long-term facility that will best meet the needs of a family can be frustrating. Fortunately, some alternative directories are available on the Web:

1. Sober.com—An online community with a directory of treatment facilities nationwide, an online formum, blogs, coaching, online chats, etc., available at *http://www.sober.com*.

2. Addiction Resource Guide—A more detailed database of selected treatment centers, intervention services, and other online information can be found at *http://www.addictionresourceguide.com*. This site includes the size of the facility, type of patient, and type of treatment.

3. Addiction Centers Directory—This site offers the opportunity to post reviews of centers and read the comments of others. It is found at *http://www.addictioncentersdirectory.com*.

4. CRC Health Group—This is one of several large private behavioral health networks with treatment centers in a number of states. Such networks use a common clearinghouse to match a patient with an appropriate facility. This may be an option for individuals with special needs, such as dual diagnosis, which may not be appropriate for most treatment centers. This network can be found at *http://www.crchealth.com*. A health insurance provider will have listings for similar networks qualified with its health plan.

5. Sober Recovery—This online community has a number of links to a range of treatment options, as well as an extensive forum. It can be found at *http://www.soberrecovery.com*.

6. National Accreditation Organizations—One accrediting organization for substance abuse treatment centers is the National Association of Addiction Treatment Providers. Their Web site at *http://www.naatp.org* provides a listing of its approximately 250 member providers.